MW00884542

1

To my father.

For teaching me to love mechanics.

4

Motorcycle mechanics

A Step-by-Step Guide to Motorcycle Maintenance and Repair

Index

1 Introduction

My first crush happened when I was 24 years old.

It was a '78 Sanglas 400F (a Spanish classic motorcycle) which had belonged to my father. It slept its last days under a dingy blanket, eaten by dust and mice.

I set out to give it a second chance. My problem: I <u>had no idea about mechanics</u>.

At that time, I would have given anything to have someone sit down with me and explain how that motorcycle worked, what its parts were and how I could fix all those problems that were keeping it at a standstill.

Above all, I would have greatly appreciated it if someone could have explained it to me in words I could understand.

No matter how hard I searched, I ended up finding explanations that were too technical for my limited knowledge, or contradictory explanations for the same problem.

The aim of this book is to explain how a motorcycle works, to tell you one by one about its parts and to talk about its breakdowns and possible solutions, but always as if it were a conversation between friends.

I am not going to go into incomprehensible technicalities that you can look up on the internet. I want to explain the **basic mechanics of a motorcycle** in words that everyone can understand.

In this book we will start from scratch, from the very basics inside a motorcycle, but we will get to the last bolt worth understanding.

I assure you that I have learned as much from writing it as I have from fixing and restoring motorcycles, so it is an honor for me to be able to tell you about it now.

I hope not to disappoint you.

Let's get started. Let's get to work.

2 How This Book is Organized

I have tried to make reading this book simple and enjoyable rather than delve into technicalities and long and tedious procedures.

Each of the book's chapters corresponds to a main part of the motorcycle.

First, the component is described, naming its main elements, its types, if any, and its most important characteristics.

Each bike is a world unto itself, so I have chosen to focus on its general characteristics, although some elements may vary from one bike to another.

After describing each of the parts, the most common breakdowns or maintenance tasks for each of these parts are reviewed.

I have focused on those tasks that you can objectively do yourself, with common household tools. Of course, there will be breakdowns that will inevitably have to be fixed in a workshop.

When you find the spark plug icon, you will be faced with a curiosity related to the topic we are dealing with.

When you find this symbol, you will be in a maintenance chapter of your motorcycle. You will find them in the corresponding section of the bike, which is to say, if it is about changing the oil, you will find it in the engine section and, if we are going to tighten the chain, it will appear in the transmission section.

At the end of the book, you will find a table with all the maintenances, depending on the miles traveled, and the corresponding page where you can find the explanation of how to do it.

The book is structured so that you can jump from chapter to chapter without having to follow an order and go to the component that interests you, without fear of having missed something important to understand that particular component.

3   Mechanical Tips

Mechanics can be a wonderful hobby that fills your spirit and the hours of your day.

You've probably had the feeling that a whole Saturday morning of fiddling with your bike has suddenly vanished.

However, here are some tips that I have learned over the years with my hands in the grease:

1)   Be realistic, or at least prudent.

It won't be the first time I think I can take a whole engine apart and put it back together in a weekend.

Finally, Sunday arrives, and the bike has to stay totally stripped down and open until I have a weekend off again.

It is preferable to be prudent and not undertake tasks that either we are not capable of doing or that clearly require more time than we have planned.

2)   Be tidy.

Carefully store any parts you disassemble during a repair, even the smallest washer.

Keep the screws with their nut and washer, if possible screwed to their part, in the same order in which they were assembled.

Take the opportunity to clean every part you disassemble.

If you find parts in bad condition, do not put them back on the bike. It's not expensive to replace a dull bolt with a new one. However, it is very expensive to have to cut apart because a bolt doesn't come out.

When disassembling parts that go together in an orderly fashion, such as transmission gears, store them in the correct order, e.g., with a wire or cable tie.

3) Ask for help.

Be aware of your limitations. There is no better way to learn than to ask for help from someone who knows more than you.

The beer afterwards will taste much better.

4) Focus.

If you are going to repair a flasher relay, don't end up changing the bike's oil.

Finish what you start and do things one at a time. You'll avoid losing pieces ... And your head!

5) Take pictures of everything.

When repairs take a long time, it is impossible to remember where the red wire went, or whether that screw had a *grower washer* or a brass washer.

Take pictures, it's free.

6) Respect the tightening torques.

For delicate parts, the manufacturer sets the torque at which the bolts must be tightened.

Trying to tighten a nut tighter than necessary will only cause it to be ruined.

Torque wrenches are available to adjust the tightening torque without overtightening.

Picture 1.   Torque wrench

If the manufacturer has not indicated the tightening torque, you can orient yourself with this table:

Thread diameter [mm]	Quality 5.8 Tightening torque [kg/m]	Quality 8.8 Tightening torque [kg/m]
4	0,2	0,38
5	0,4	0,76
6	0,8	1,3
8	1,6	3,1
10	4,0	6,2
12	7,0	10,0
14	11,2	17,3
16	17,5	27,0
20	34,1	52,7
24	58,8	91,4

7) **Use quality tools.**

It may seem silly, but a bad screwdriver or a bad flat wrench can ruin any nut or bolt.

8) Patience, heat, hammer and 3 in 1.

There is no locked screw that can resist such an infallible combination.

Apply 3 in 1. Give a few blows with the hammer and try again. As many times as necessary.

If nothing works, try a blowtorch or a hair dryer, sometimes it works like a charm.

9) Don't skimp on gaskets or filters.

Whenever you open and find gaskets, replace them. They are designed to seal when they are new. Once they are deformed, they usually do not fulfill their function.

Do not save on filters either, they are not expensive and their function is vital. If you change the oil, always change the filter.

10) Before mounting, grease.

All internal parts of the engine and all bearings need greasing. Before closing it again, apply a good dose of grease.

11) Do not reuse press-fitted parts.

Never use press-fitted parts: seals, grower washers, circlips, metal gaskets.

They have lost their initial shape and are now worthless.

Its price is negligible, do not gamble.

4 Parts of a Motorcycle

Before starting, it is important to have a general outline of the components of a motorcycle.

In each of the chapters we will analyze them in much more detail, however, before studying a component in depth, we might want to have an idea of where it is, right?

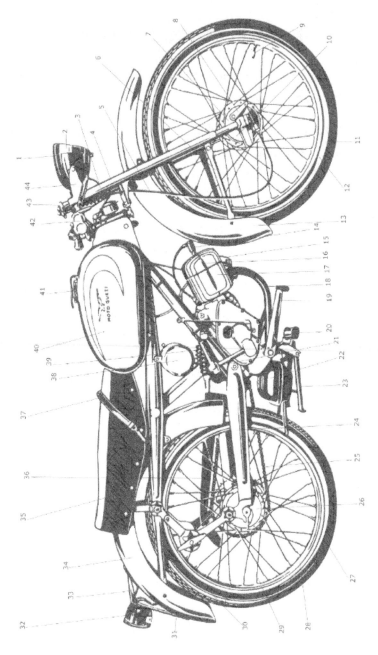

Picture 2.   Parts of a motorcycle

18

1. Headlight
2. Headlamp bezel
3. Horn
4. Fork bar
5. Front brake cable
6. Fender brace
7. Front drum brake
8. Drum brake cam
9. Tire nipple
10. Wheel hub
11. Front tire
12. Rear tire
13. Front fender
14. Spark plug pipe
15. Air filter and carburetor

16. Stock
17. Engine (cylinder)
18. Exhaust pipe
19. Gear pedal
20. Footrest rubber
21. Starter pedal
22. Oil reservoir
23. Kickstand
24. Swingarm
25. Chain
26. Rear hub
27. Rear tire
28. Rear rim
29. Spokes
30. Subframe

31. License plate
32. Rear light
33. License plate holder
34. Rear fender
35. Seat
36. Chain cover
37. Seat belt
38. Toolbox
39. Swingarm shock absorber
40. Gasoline tank
41. Tank cap
42. Throttle grip
43. Handlebar
44. Headlamp bracket

5 Starting the Motorcycle

I wanted to start talking about mechanics at the beginning.

It all starts with starting your bike, or at least that's what we always believe.

If you have ever restored a motorcycle, you will know that the first thing your body asks you to do is to start it. Everything else takes a back seat. If the bike starts, then nothing is impossible.

The same thing happens when we buy a motorcycle. Seeing it at the dealership or in the hands of its owner is all very well, but we want to start it, to hear it.

Mechanical problems will come later.

Something as simple as starting our motorcycle, which today we do by pressing a simple button, has been a headache for our ancestors for years.

To start the bike is to provoke the first explosion, the first engine turn, the first spark. Once the engine is turning, the spark plug creating sparks and the mixture exploding, the engine will move by itself, but the first time you will have to help it.

To generate this first turn, there are essentially two systems: the starter pedal and the starter motor.

5.1 The starter pedal

The starter pedal is nothing more than a crank with which, by applying force with the foot, we will set in motion a series of gears that will ultimately move the piston of the motorcycle, starting its movement.

Our leg generates the necessary force to start the engine cycle, which, once it starts producing explosions, will move autonomously.

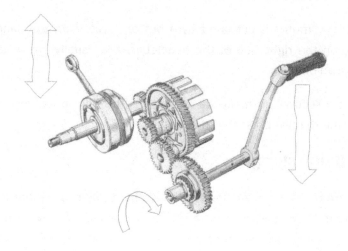

Picture 3.   Starter pedal

Another starting system with exactly the same rationale as the starter pedal is the kick starter, typical on many older mopeds such as the Vespino.

In this case, instead of one starter pedal, we will have two, as if it were a bicycle. Moving the pedals with a gear engaged will start the engine.

5.2   The starter motor

Nowadays it is not common for motorcycles to be started mechanically, by means of a starter pedal. Convenience has prevailed and it is rare to find a motorcycle that does not have a starter motor.

The rationale of the starter motor is exactly the same: to cause the engine to start moving until it moves on its own.

In this case, instead of the leg making the effort, an electric motor, which must be powered by the battery, will do it. This electric motor, by means of gears, transmits its rotation to the crankshaft.

The starter motor is activated by a button located on the handlebar, usually on the right side of the handlebar, and usually has a lightning bolt drawn on it.

To start a scooter normally we must press the right brake lever at the same time that we press the start button.

5.3 Bump start

There are times when we have no choice but to start our motorcycle by pushing it. If we do not have a starter pedal and we have run out of battery, we will have no other option.

To do this, we will cause the piston to move by means of the gearbox itself.

The mechanism is very easy to explain and its difficulty to carry out in practice depends on the weight and height of the motorcycle, the existence or not of downhill slopes and the skill of the driver.

We will start the movement with the key in the ignition position and the second gear engaged. We will squeeze the clutch lever, otherwise we will not be able to move the motorcycle. We will force the motorcycle to move, helping us with a slope or pushing it.

When the motorcycle has reached a sufficient speed, release the clutch. The motorcycle should start.

When the engine is running and we engage a gear, the wheel moves, starting the movement. The rationale behind this method is to achieve the opposite, to force the engine to move by turning the wheel.

First gear is not used because it is the gear that requires the most force to move the wheel, so when releasing the clutch, the bike would slow down a lot.

5.4   Common malfunctions: my bike doesn't start

Starting a motorcycle is a result of all systems (or at least most of them) functioning correctly.

In other words, if a motorcycle does not start, the causes can be almost infinite.

It is important to differentiate between your motorcycle not starting when it did the night before, or you have just bought a motorcycle that has been stationary for 20 years and, logically, it won't start.

Causes of a motorcycle that was working yesterday doesn't start

a)   Is the lock button pressed?

It sounds silly, but it wouldn't be the first time I've borrowed a bike and been told that it suddenly won't start.

The first check (a bit silly, I know) you should make is whether the lock or emergency stop button is pressed.

It is usually red, with a crossed-out circular arrow and located on the right handlebar grip.

Picture 4.   Start lock button

b) The kickstand is not removed

Today's motorcycles (and have been for many years) have a safety feature that locks the ignition when the kickstand is engaged.

If the motorcycle is on its center stand, it should start.

If the kickstand spring has lost its force and the kickstand does not return to its retracted position, it may lock the ignition.

Try to push it with your hand and press the start button.

c) Have you tightened the lever?

Sorry for the basics, but I want to rule out all possible "silly" bugs first.

Most scooters and some other motorcycles are started by pressing the starter button and the brake or clutch lever at the same time.

If you are not doing this your bike will not start.

d) The motorcycle has a proximity key

The most modern and high-end motorcycles can be fitted with a proximity key starter, i.e., without the need to insert it into the cylinder.

This system can be altered by frequency inhibitors.

If you live in a big city, near embassies or government buildings, you may not be able to start your motorcycle normally.

Drag the bike a few meters out of the inhibitor's area of influence and it will start without any problems.

e) The motorcycle has no battery

This is the most common cause of a motorcycle not starting.

A battery can last about 2 to 3 years and, although it warns us, we tend to overlook those extra seconds it takes for the bike to start every day.

One morning, all of a sudden, the battery says enough is enough and there is not enough capacity to activate the starter motor.

We will notice that we have run out of battery when the bike makes at least an attempt to start. The lights and horn may work (sometimes it will be more quiet than usual), but the starter motor, which needs much more voltage, will eventually stall.

The solution is to buy a new battery. If you suspect that it may be due to an electrical leak, you can charge it with a battery charger (and fix the leak).

You can try to bump start the bike. Once started, if the battery is not "dead" it will be charged by your bike's alternator.

Having a portable jump starter (a small battery with enough capacity to drive the starter motor) also helps.

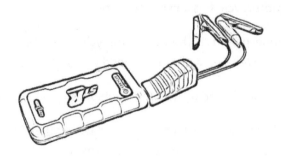

Picture 5.   Portable starter

f) Bad connection at battery or starter motor

If the bike literally "does nothing", i.e., no lights, horn and, of course, the starter motor does not make any attempt to move, it is likely that some contact is wrong.

In that case, provided that the design of your bike allows it, locate the cables coming out of the battery and check that they are connected and do not move easily. Do the same with the cable feeding the starter motor.

If you cannot access the wiring or the bike is still not showing signs of life you will have to check the installation thoroughly.

If your bike has a fuse box (it does, but whether it is accessible is another matter), check for a blown fuse. It is as easy as replacing it.

Picture 6.   Fuse in good condition, melted and burned out

g) The bike is "cold".

When a motorcycle has not been used for a while, it is common for it not to start on the first try, especially in cold weather.

Fluids need some temperature to flow properly through all their conduits, and that's not easy to achieve if your bike sleeps on the street and the weather is cold.

We can only be patient and pray that we don't drain the battery in the attempt.

If your bike has an air lever or starter, it is time to use it.

Its function is to throttle the passage of air so that the mixture entering the cylinder is richer in gasoline, and therefore explodes more easily.

h) Spark plug

Another classic cause that prevents a motorcycle from starting properly is the condition of the spark plug.

Frequently check its color and geometry, to make sure that it is not due to be changed.

I recommend that you always carry a rag on the bike and a spark plug wrench, it will get you out of a lot of trouble.

Simply unscrew, clean and replace.

In the chapter dedicated to spark plugs I show you all the possible failures.

Causes of a motorcycle that has not been running for years that will not start

When we buy an old motorcycle, or one that has not been used for years, or when we try to start a motorcycle that we had left sleeping for years in a garage, the most common thing is that it does not start.

The causes can be infinite, starting with all those described in the previous section.

In order not to list all the breakdowns of a motorcycle, I propose to reduce it to the following decision chart:

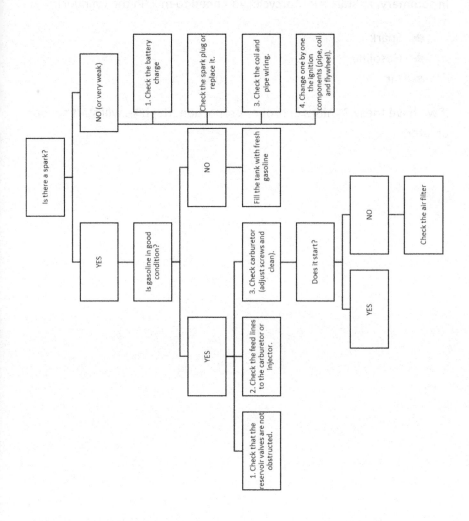

Is there a spark?

- YES
- NO (or very weak)

NO (or very weak):
1. Check the battery charge
2. Check the spark plug or replace it.
3. Check the coil and pipe wiring.
4. Change one by one the ignition components (pipe, coil and flywheel).

YES → Is gasoline in good condition?
- YES
- NO

NO: Fill the tank with fresh gasoline

YES:
1. Check that the reservoir valves are not obstructed.
2. Check the feed lines to the carburetor or injector.
3. Check carburetor (adjust screws and clean).

Does it start?
- YES
- NO

NO: Check the air filter

If after checking all this the bike still doesn't start you will have to keep reading, because there is probably some other problem.

In summary, to start a motorcycle, you need to mix (in the cylinder):

- 🏍 Spark
- 🏍 Gasoline
- 🏍 Air

If we have these 3 things in proper proportion, the bike will start sooner or later.

6 The Engine

The engine is the component that moves the motorcycle. Probably the most important and complex.

Although they are becoming more and more different, they were originally very similar to car engines. In fact, sometimes engines were interchanged between motorcycles and cars.

Such was the case in the 1960s in the UK, where Norton motorcycle engines were highly sought after for car racing. This caused an important supply of Norton chassis without engines, which were used to install Triumph Bonneville engines, creating a unique motorcycle, with the union of both brands as a name: "Triton". This bike was one of the most legendary Cafe Racers.

Picture 7.   Triton Motorcycle

Another substantial difference between car and motorcycle engines is fuel. While in cars, apart from electric cars, the market is divided between diesel and gasoline, the vast majority of motorcycle engines are gasoline.

In the engine, the energy caused by the explosion of the air-gasoline mixture is converted into motion of the motorcycle.

To cause the explosion, we need a spark, which is caused by the spark plug. The result of this explosion, in addition to this energy, are gases that are expelled through the exhaust pipe.

Air + gasoline + spark = energy (movement) + gases

To name the union of air and gasoline they did not break their heads too much and called it a mixture.

The mixture comes from the carburetor or the injectors, but this will be discussed in the chapter on engine fueling.

6.1 Engine parts

In the following diagram you can see the most important parts of a motor.

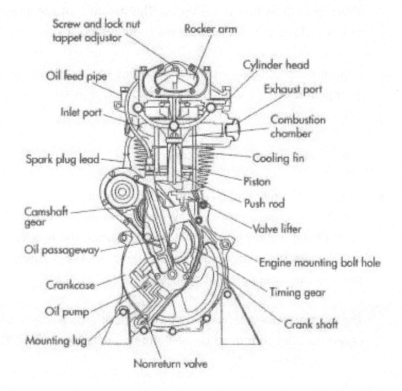

Picture 8.   Engine parts

These parts, as well as their particularities for each type of motorcycle, are explained below.

I have tried not to leave out any important component, but I admit that I have had to leave some out to avoid running out of readers right at the beginning of the book.

   🏍 **Cylinder**: is the metallic compartment containing the piston, as its name suggests, it is cylindrical in shape. If an engine were a syringe, the cylinder would be the outer part that does not move.

The cylinder marks the capacity of the engine, so we talk about 250cc or quarter-liter motorcycles. This means that the internal capacity of the cylinder is 250 cubic centimeters.

A motorcycle can have one or more cylinders, and these can be arranged in line, in V, or facing each other, as is the case with BMW *boxer* engines.

The cylinder sits on the **crankcase**.

🏍 **Piston**: it is a metallic piece (made of aluminum) that goes up and down inside the cylinder. When the explosion occurs, the force of the explosion pushes it down, starting the mechanism that moves the motorcycle. In the simile of the syringe, the piston is the inner part that pushes the liquid (plunger).

The piston moves between two limit positions, a lower one, called BDC (bottom dead center) and an upper one, called TDC (top dead center).

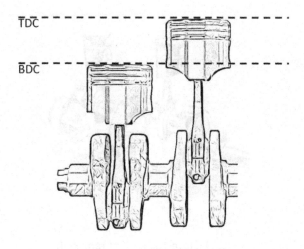

Picture 9.   TDC and BDC

🏍 The **piston skirt is the part of the piston** that is below its connection with the connecting rod. This joint is called a piston pin and is nothing more than the through cylinder perpendicular to the connecting rod.

🏍 **Cylinder head**: is the cover that closes the cylinder at the top, housing the combustion chamber. It is the highest part of the engine.

There is nothing more typical than hearing that the cylinder head gasket has a failure. It is nothing more than a rubber or paper that keeps the chamber that closes the cylinder head perfectly watertight.

🏍 **Crankshaft**: it is the element in charge of transforming the vertical movement (up and down) of the piston into a rotary movement (like the wheels). The crankshaft is a part that only rotates without stopping.

Picture 10.   Crankshaft

The part of the crankshaft where the connecting rod is attached is called the **crankpin**.

🏍 **Connecting rod**: if the cylinder goes up and down without stopping, and the crankshaft rotates without stopping, we need a component that links both movements. It is none other than the connecting rod.

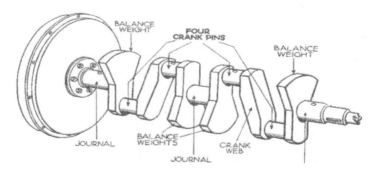

Picture 11.   Crankshaft parts

- 🏍 **Spark plug**: it is in charge of creating the spark that causes the explosion.
- 🏍 **Combustion chamber**: is the space between the top of the piston, when it is at its TDC, and the cylinder head. The explosion that moves everything takes place in this space.

Picture 12.   Combustion chamber

- 🏍 **Valves**: we will find them only in 4-stroke engines. They are in charge of opening and closing the combustion chamber. We will have at least 2 per cylinder, one that lets the mixture of air and gasoline coming from the carburetor or the injectors, called intake valve, and another one that lets out the gases caused by the explosion, called exhaust valve.

It is common, in modern engines, to find cylinders with more than two valves. Thus, we can have a cylinder with 2 intake valves and 2 exhaust valves, 3 intake valves and 2 exhaust valves or other configurations.

It used to be very common in the advertising of car brands to emphasize that it had 16 valves (16v). This meant that the car had a 4-cylinder engine with 4 valves per cylinder, 2 intake and 2 exhaust valves. This type of engine had a sportier behavior, although, on the contrary, they consumed more.

The valves are located at the top of the engine, at the head of the cylinder head.

Picture 13.   Motorcycle valves

🏍 **Cams**: Cams are the parts that open and close valves. If the valve is a door, the cams are the doorknob. The total number of cams in the engine together form the so-called camshaft.

Picture 14.   Cam

The cams have a specific geometry so that, as they rotate with the crankshaft, they open and close the valves.

The cams are also moved by the crankshaft, which is not only responsible for moving the pistons. The way the cams are moved from the crankshaft is what we know as timing.

Picture 15.   Scooter camshaft

- **Rocker arms**: the cams themselves do not open the valves (with the exception of some engines) but send the order to the rocker arms.

They are so called because of their movement, similar to a seesaw. If we imagine two children on the floor, the one who is leaning on the floor would push the valve with his feet, opening it.

At the end of each rocker arm, there is a screw that allows to regulate the valve opening degree. These are the so-called tappets, which we will mention later to learn how to make the famous tappet adjustment.

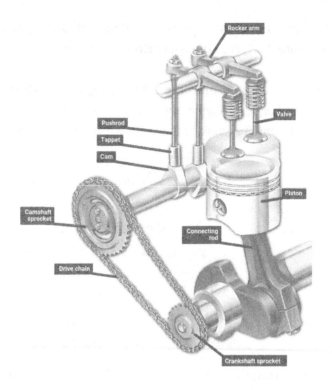

Picture 16.   Rocker arm operation

The cams are moved by the crankshaft itself, through a chain or gears.

By the way, like valves, you will only find them on 4-stroke engines. If there are no valves there is no need to open and close them.

🏍 **Cylinder liner**: the so-called cylinder liner is nothing more than a lining of its inner wall. Since it has a metal part inside that keeps going up and down rubbing against the wall (the piston), it is usually made of a more resistant material. There are jacketed cylinders and unjacketed cylinders, in which the piston rubs directly against the inside wall of the cylinder.

When we talk about cylinder reboring, we refer to the replacement of the cylinder liner or the installation of a new one on top of the old damaged one.

🏍 **Piston rings**: there must be a minimum clearance between the piston and the cylinder liner, otherwise it would not be possible to move one inside the other.

To prevent the oil in the lower part of the cylinder from mixing with the gasoline in the upper part and to make the combustion chamber as airtight as possible, flexible metal parts are incorporated between the piston and the cylinder liner.

There are normally three. The two upper ones are responsible for sealing the cylinder to prevent the passage of gases and liquids. The lower one, called the oil scraper ring, is responsible for lubricating the cylinder liner. Another of its functions is to transmit heat from the piston to the cylinder.

They are not interchangeable; each has a unique section according to its function.

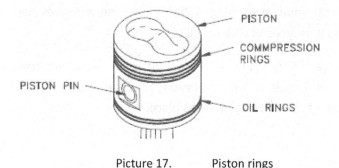

Picture 17.   Piston rings

- **Fins**: it is very common to find on the outside of the cylinders, fins or metal sheets. Their function is to allow air to circulate through them as we move forward, in order to cool the engine. When the fins are not sufficient, as is usually the case with scooters or large displacement motorcycles, a radiator is installed in front of the cylinder, so that the air passing through it can cool the engine.

- **Crankcase:** the crankcase is the support of the engine, the fixed structure on which the rest of the components are installed. It occupies the lower part of the block and serves as a container for the gearbox and the oils that lubricate the entire engine. It is also where the crankshaft is supported. Crankcase, cylinders and cylinder heads form the fixed part of the engine, its enclosure and support.

  The crankcase can be dry or wet, depending on the type of engine lubrication. This will be discussed later.

- **Studs**: these are the through bolts that close the whole assembly.

6.2 The cylinder

The cylinder (and everything it houses) is the essential part of the engine, so it deserves a chapter all to itself.

As we have briefly explained before, it is the part that contains the piston, and inside it the explosion that eventually generates the movement of the motorcycle takes place.

Displacement

The first aspect to deal with, speaking of cylinders, as the name suggests, is the **displacement.**

The displacement of an engine is the capacity or volume of its cylinders and is measured in cubic centimeters (cc). This volume is determined by the cylinder bore and the **piston stroke** (distance between TDC and BDC).

$$Displacement\ of\ a\ cylinder = \frac{\pi * Diameter^2}{4} * Stroke$$

The total displacement of an engine is the sum of the volume of all its cylinders.

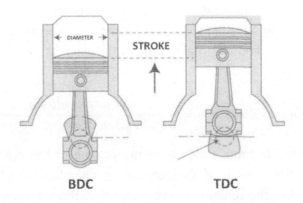

Picture 18.   Displacement

In the simile with the syringe, the displacement is equivalent to the capacity (in cubic centimeters) of the syringe. It depends on the internal diameter of the syringe and the distance traveled by the internal piston (stroke).

It is understandable that the larger the capacity of a cylinder, the greater the amount of mixture that fits inside it, and therefore the more

43

powerful its explosion will be. A large stove heats more than a small stove, right?

Compression ratio

Another magnitude of vital importance in the study of a cylinder is its compression ratio: it measures how much we manage to compress the mixture of gasoline and air inside the cylinder.

As we have explained, the maximum volume of a cylinder is achieved when the piston is at its lowest point (Bottom Dead Center or BDC), and the minimum volume when it is at its highest point (Top Dead Center or TDC). At this point, there is still a small space between the top face of the piston and the cylinder head, known as the combustion chamber.

The compression ratio is the ratio between the volume of the combustion chamber (that small volume left by the piston when it is at its highest point) and the total volume of the cylinder (when the piston is at the bottom).

$$Compression\ ratio = \frac{Cylinder\ volume}{Combustion\ chamber\ volume}$$

It is measured in times one, i.e., if the volume of the cylinder were 250cc and the volume of the combustion chamber was 25cc, then 250/25=10, i.e., the volume of the cylinder is 10 times greater than that of the combustion chamber, so the ratio is 10:1.

Caution, in the above example, cylinder capacity should not be confused with cylinder volume. If the cylinder volume is 250cc and the combustion chamber volume is 25cc, the cylinder capacity would be 250cc-25cc=225cc, i.e., the combustion **chamber is not taken into account when calculating the cylinder capacity.**

Generally speaking, the higher the compression ratio, the more power we get.

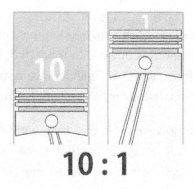

10 : 1

Picture 19.   Compression ratio

Number of cylinders

At first, for technical reasons, the engines had only one cylinder, that is, they were single cylinder. It is obvious to think that, if with one cylinder we obtain a certain force, with two cylinders we obtain twice the force, and with three cylinders, therefore, we will obtain three times the force.

This is not exactly so; however, it is true that, with a greater number of equal cylinders, we will obtain a superior force, and for this reason engines with more cylinders were appearing. Thus, we find two-cylinder, three-cylinder, four-cylinder, etc. engines.

In fact, nowadays, only small-displacement motorcycles are single-cylinder. In fact, the unit displacement of a cylinder does not usually exceed 250cc.

For the same displacement, an engine with several cylinders will be more powerful than a single cylinder. That is to say, if I have a 500cc motorcycle, I will get more power by spreading the displacement over two 250cc cylinders than with a single 500cc cylinder.

In addition to power, multi-cylinder engines are easier to start, have less vibration and behave more smoothly than a single-cylinder engine.

On the other hand, a larger number of cylinders makes the engine more expensive and more difficult to maintain.

Let us imagine an army in which strength is measured by the weight of its soldiers. Under general circumstances, we would agree that it would be more profitable to have a troop of 3 soldiers weighing 50 kg, than a single soldier weighing 150 kg.

Indeed, as we increase the size of a single cylinder, its inertia increases, and it becomes necessary to strengthen the entire system to support such a powerful cylinder.

> *The record for the number of cylinders in a motorcycle engine is held by the British Simon Whitlock. He has built a motorcycle with a 2-stroke engine that has 48 cylinders and a capacity of 4200 cc. It consists of 16 Kawasaki KH250 3-cylinder engines arranged in six banks of eight and is completely road legal (according to him). The engine is so big that it has a complete single-cylinder 2-stroke engine to serve as a starter motor.*

Arrangement

In motorcycles with more than one cylinder, these can be arranged in line, in V or facing each other (BMW twin-cylinder *boxer* type).

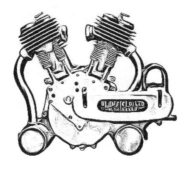

Picture 20.   V-Engine

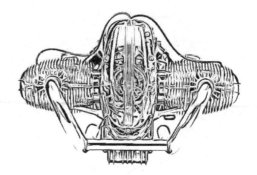

Picture 21.   BMW boxer engine

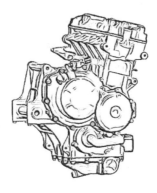

Picture 22.   Inline or Straight engine

The arrangement of the cylinders is part of the design of each brand, and influences such important characteristics as cooling (the more exposed they are, the better they will cool) or the position of the crankshaft (with in-line cylinders, the crankshaft will be positioned perpendicular to the direction of travel, with opposed cylinders, the crankshaft will be positioned parallel to the direction of travel, and with V-cylinders, both configurations are possible).

The cylinder arrangement must also take into account the final size of the engine. Boxer engines are very wide, so they must be mounted higher to avoid rubbing the cylinder heads in a curve.

6.3   Types of motorcycle engines

The 4-stroke engine

The 4-stroke gasoline engine, as we know it today, was invented by the German Otto. It takes its name from the number of stages or strokes the piston needs to complete a full cycle.

It is the most common engine that exists in motorcycles. It is also the engine that drives the vast majority of gasoline-powered cars.

The four times are:

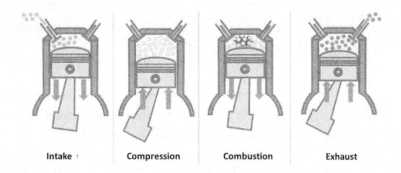

Intake   Compression   Combustion   Exhaust

Picture 23.   Stages of a 4-stroke engine

1. Intake

The piston is lowered, and the intake valve is open. This causes the inlet (intake) of mixture (gasoline+air) coming from the carburetor or injector.

2. Compression

The piston rises. The two valves are closed so that the mixture that has entered the intake stage cannot escape and is compressed between the piston head and the cylinder head.

This compression of the mixture causes it to increase in pressure and temperature. It is ready to explode.

3. Explosion or combustion

When the piston has reached its highest point (Top Dead Center or TDC), the spark plug generates a spark and the air-gasoline mixture explodes. The force generated by the explosion forces the piston downward. Both valves remain closed.

> *In reality, the spark is produced an instant before the piston reaches its highest point. This instant is known as ignition advance and will be discussed in the chapter on ignition.*

This is the most important of the four phases, in which the movement that moves the motorcycle is generated.

4. Exhaust

The piston rises again, but this time the exhaust valve is open, so the piston itself pushes out the gases produced in the explosion.

When the piston reaches its highest point (TDC), the exhaust valve closes and the intake valve opens, starting the cycle again.

Throughout this cycle, the piston makes four strokes inside the cylinder, two upward and two downward, and the crankshaft makes two complete revolutions.

> *It should be pointed out that this is an ideal operation, so that it is easy to understand. However, in reality, and especially when the bike is running at high rpm, neither the spark is produced just at TDC (advance to ignition), nor when the exhaust valve closes the intake valve opens (there are times when both are open, this is known as crossover), nor does the exhaust valve open just at BDC (it opens a little before reaching BDC).*
>
> *However, the operation is valid, as I say, to understand the cycle of a 4-stroke engine.*
>
> *The true operating cycle is known as the practical or real cycle, as opposed to this ideal, which would be the theoretical cycle.*

The 2-stroke engine

Two-stroke engines, although less and less frequent, have coexisted with 4-stroke engines since the invention of the motorcycle. In fact, until very recently, the vast majority of low-displacement motorcycles were fitted with two-stroke engines, as they are much simpler and cheaper.

If the name of the 4-stroke engine indicated that its complete cycle comprised 4 phases (intake, compression, combustion and exhaust), obviously a 2-stroke engine has only two phases ... or does it?

Beware of this tricky question. In a 2-stroke engine, **the 4 phases** of the Otto cycle **also occur.**

The difference is that, if in the 4-stroke engine, to complete a cycle the piston had to rise twice, with two turns of the crankshaft, in a 2-stroke engine the piston only rises once, and the crankshaft makes only one turn. That is, in a 2-stroke engine, the cycle is completed with two piston strokes.

Another of the most notable differences of the 2-stroke engine is that it has no valves.

It is the piston itself in its path inside the cylinder that opens and closes the openings (called ports) that give access to the mixture and let the gases escape. With this we save the entire distribution installation, which is one of the most complex of a 4-stroke engine.

Parts of a 2-stroke engine

Although most of the parts coincide with a 4-stroke engine, which was seen in the previous section, a 2-stroke engine has some components that deserve to be explained if we want to understand its operation.

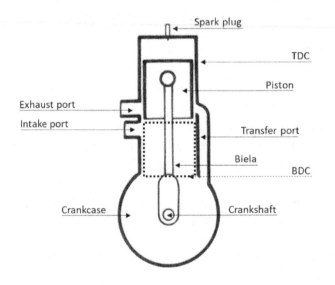

Picture 24.   Parts of a 2-stroke engine

The first difference that at this point should catch our attention in the above picture is the absence of valves at the top of the cylinder.

Indeed, a 2-stroke cylinder has no valves. On the other hand, there are 3 conduits that did not exist in the 4-stroke engine: the ports.

The ports perform the same functions as the valves in a 4-stroke engine.

- The intake port is the duct that allows the mixture to enter (in this case the mixture, in addition to air and gasoline, includes oil, although we will see this later).
- The exhaust port allows the combustion gases to escape.
- Special mention should be made of the transfer port, which is responsible for transferring the intake gases from the crankcase to the top of the cylinder and thus helps to push the exhaust gases through the corresponding port.

Let's analyze the piston stroke inside the cylinder.

We start from the position of the piston at its highest point, the Top Dead Center or TDC. At this point, the mixture is fully compressed, and the spark is produced at the spark plug, which will trigger the whole process.

We can see how the piston has left the intake port door free, which the mixture takes advantage of to flood the part under the piston, which we can call the crankcase.

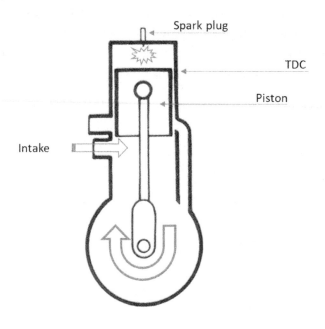

Picture 25.   2T piston at TDC. Combustion phase

After the explosion, the piston descends with force, closing the intake port on its way and opening the exhaust port, a fact that will be used by the gases to leave the combustion chamber through the exhaust port.

It can be seen how the space in the crankcase, where the mixture is already waiting, is reduced by the effect of the lowering of the piston. This causes the precompression of the mixture in the crankcase.

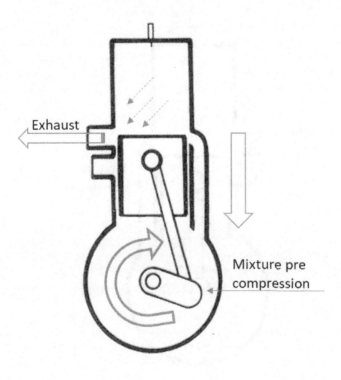

Exhaust

Mixture pre compression

Picture 26.   2-stroke exhaust phase

The piston continues to descend and opens the door to the transfer port, at which point the mixture, which was running out of space in the crankcase, escapes into the combustion chamber above the piston. This transfer helps to evacuate the combustion gases remaining in the cylinder.

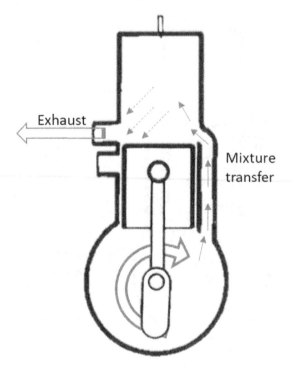

Picture 27.   Intake phase

The piston rises again and closes the exhaust and transfer ports as it passes through, thus creating a hermetic chamber, full of mixture, which will be compressed waiting for a spark that will blow everything apart.

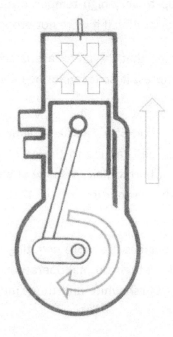

Picture 28.   Compression phase

By the way, if you have noticed, we have completed all the phases of the cycle in a single turn of the crankshaft, whereas, for a 4-stroke cycle, it would take two complete turns.

How is a two-stroke cylinder lubricated?

A piston of a 2-stroke engine moves up and down in the cylinder without stopping, just like the piston of a 4-stroke motorcycle. Therefore, it heats up to very high temperatures that would cause its deformation and deterioration if it were not properly lubricated.

However, we have seen that the crankcase is occupied by the mixture and is used to precompress it, so it cannot be filled with oil as it is in a 4-stroke engine.

This is why the lubrication of a 2-stroke engine is carried out directly with the mixture, i.e., oil is added to the gasoline tank so that, when passing through the carburetor, air, gasoline and oil are introduced into the cylinder. It is this proportion of oil that lubricates the piston (approximately 2%).

This is why 2-stroke engines are more polluting than 4-stroke engines, because they burn oil in their normal operation. This also causes their exhaust smoke to be bluish-white and they smell much more than 4-stroke motorcycles.

Comparison between a 2-stroke and a 4-stroke engine

In a quick comparison between a 4-stroke engine and a 2-stroke engine we have that:

	4-stroke	2-stroke
Number of phases	4	4
Crankshaft revolutions per cycle	2	1
Piston strokes per cycle	4	2
Number of valves	Minimum 2 per cylinder	No valves
Consumption	Less	More
Power	Less	More
Performance	More	Less
Contamination	Less	More
Price	More	Less

The electric engine

Something totally unthinkable a few years ago but which is becoming more and more common in our streets is the presence of electric motorcycles.

On an electric motorcycle everything is much simpler. The energy is stored in a battery and transmitted to an electric motor.

The operation of an electric engine (whether it is a motorcycle or a mixer) consists of a static component and another component that rotates around it.

The static component consists of copper wire windings and is called a stator. When an electric current is passed through these windings (small copper wires), a magnetic field is generated.

This magnetic field produces the rotation of the other spinning component, called the rotor.

From this point on, the operation is the same as in any other engine: by means of gears we manage to move a wheel.

6.4   The engine lubrication system

We have already talked about pistons. Imagine a steel cylinder inside a steel tube, up and down more than 5,000 times per minute. The best thing that could happen is that it would melt from the heat caused by the friction between the two metals. The noise would be unbearable. The heat would be scorching.

Our bike would leave the dealership, after having spent a small fortune (or not so small), to last us a few meters.

To avoid this tragedy, the lubrication system was invented.

It is nothing more (and nothing less) than a mechanism in charge of supplying oil to the metal parts that are forced to constantly rub against each other, as is the case of the pistons inside the cylinder.

In addition to helping to lubricate the joints between different metals, oils and greases have other - although not less important - functions:

- **Cooling function**: oils contribute to lowering the temperature of parts not reached by the engine's cooling system.
- **Cleaning function**: grease and oil carry away impurities that have penetrated the engine or remains of worn components that settle to the bottom of the crankcase or filters.

> *Try putting a coin near the oil cap of the crankcase, you will see how it sticks. The oil plugs incorporate a magnet to trap small metallic debris that comes off the engine.*

- 🏍 **Neutralizing function**: during combustion, acid residues are generated, which can corrode the metal parts that make up the engine. Oils are responsible for neutralizing these residues.
- 🏍 **Sealing function**: the oil ensures the sealing of the combustion chamber by creating a film that prevents gases from escaping from the top of the piston.

How is the engine lubricated?

In 4-stroke engines, the oil is incorporated into the crankcase, which is the receptacle located in the lower part of the engine. From there, it is carried to the rest of the engine, normally by means of crankshaft driven pumps or by the "oil mist" effect, which is nothing more than the splashing that occurs in the crankcase with the movement of its interior components. This type of lubrication is called **wet sump**.

Occasionally, the gearbox is lubricated differently, as it requires a higher viscosity. In these cases, two types of oil are added (and changed) in separate receptacles.

On some motorcycles there is a separate oil reservoir, from which oil is circulated to the rest of the engine by pumps. This system is known as **dry sump**.

The parts in charge of transmitting the oil to its final destination are called bearings, and they have grooves through which the oil circulates, smearing each metallic element.

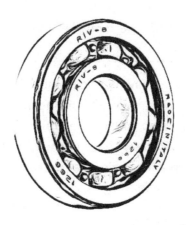

Picture 29.   Ball bearing

All 4-stroke motorcycles have an oil filter, which is responsible for collecting the impurities that have been dragging the oil on its way through the engine. It must be changed every time the oil is changed.

Lubrication in two-stroke engines

In 2-stroke engines, the mixture is usually made in the gasoline tank itself (that is why the smoke from their exhausts smells different and is more bluish, because they "burn oil", besides being much more polluting). Every time you fill up with gasoline, you will have to add a proportion of oil marked by the manufacturer, which is usually 2% of the amount of gasoline you add.

This type of lubrication is not as effective as that used in 4-stroke motorcycles, so bearings are usually used in moving parts, such as crankshaft shafts. Bearings are parts in which friction is reduced in rotating contacts by means of greased balls or elongated cylinders, which have a larger contact surface (needle cages).

If in doubt, when it comes to oiling a two-stroke motorcycle, it is better to overfill than to underfill.

There are more modern two-stroke motorcycles that have a separate reservoir connected to a small pump (driven by the crankshaft), which doses the oil needed by the engine.

The light of the oil

It is common (and recommended) to have an oil pressure indicator light on the motorcycle frame.

This light comes on when the ignition is turned on and must be turned off immediately. If it comes on while riding, you must stop quickly, or you may cause serious damage to the motorcycle.

The **oil pressure switch is** responsible for the operation of this important light. It is a part with a pusher that closes an electrical circuit. If the oil has adequate pressure, it pushes the plunger which interrupts an electrical circuit that connects to the indicator light, so the indicator goes out. If the oil does not have enough pressure to push the plunger (because there is not enough, for example), the circuit is closed, and the bulb lights up.

Why is there a tube coming out of the engine and into my air filter?

It is very common, especially on older motorcycles where the fairing plastics do not hide everything, to find a rubber tube coming out of the top of the crankcase and ending at the air filter.

This is an oil gas breather. As mentioned above, the oil forms a mist that lubricates all engine components. In addition, in its cooling function, it raises its temperature a lot when the motorcycle is running.

All this generates quite polluting gases that struggle to leave the engine. This is what this duct is for, allowing them to escape, while preventing them from being released freely into the atmosphere. In addition, they serve to preheat the intake air, improving its performance.

What do the acronyms of motorcycle oils stand for?

The oils used for engine lubrication are classified according to their viscosity grade. The Society of Automotive Engineers (S.A.E.) is responsible for this.

The higher the viscosity grade (ability to flow), the higher the number accompanying the letters SAE. For example, an SAE90 oil is much more viscous than an SAE15.

It is important to note that the viscosity grade decreases as the temperature rises, i.e., as the motorcycle warms up (or if it is summer) the oil will be more fluid. This is not beneficial as the oil does not remain adhered to the metal surfaces, but "drips" into the crankcase.

To avoid this effect, there are oils with a higher viscosity index (note that we are no longer talking about viscosity grade but about index). An oil with a high viscosity INDEX is one that varies little in fluidity as the temperature changes, i.e., it is a more stable oil.

When we start our motorcycle when it is cold, it is preferable for the oil to be very fluid, so that it circulates quickly to all the components of the engine. However, as the motorcycle heats up, what we are interested in is that the oil is more viscous and impregnates these components. This is achieved with so-called multigrade oils, which vary their viscosity as the temperature increases, because they have viscous additives that dissolve in the oil at higher temperatures.

In this case, they are named with two codes, separated by the W (for Winter, which expresses the cold viscosity), e.g., SAE 10W-40.

Picture 30.   Multigrade oil

Oils that have only one viscosity grade are called monograde (e.g., *SAE 40*).

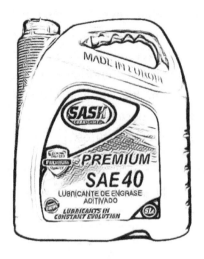

Picture 31.   Monograde oil

Summarizing:

- 🏍 **Viscosity grade**: indicates an oil's ability to flow.
- 🏍 **Viscosity index**: indicates how easy it is for an oil to change its viscosity when the temperature varies.

Synthetic or mineral oil

Mineral oils are obtained through physical processes of petroleum distillation. Synthetic oils, on the other hand, are obtained by chemical processes.

Synthetics take the lead in terms of properties, as they are much more stable (they have a much higher viscosity INDEX than minerals) and durable.

However, they are more expensive than mineral oils, which is why semi-synthetic oils, composed of homogeneous mixtures of both types of oils, are usually marketed.

⚒ Checking the oil level

Although it may seem too simple a task, it is without a doubt the most important task in motorcycle maintenance.

An oversight in checking the oil level can ruin an engine by overheating and, in the worst case, by seizure. This is aggravated if our motorcycle does not have an oil temperature or oil pressure warning light.

To check the oil level of the engine we will use the oil cap itself, through which we refill this. It usually has a protrusion at the end of the thread (sometimes, as in the BMW boxer, there is a real dipstick). We will only have to unscrew the oil cap, clean it with a rag and put it back in the hole, without screwing it, simply inserting it without forcing it as far as the thread will let you. Later we will take it out and we will observe if the oil has stained the plug inside the two lines of the end of the appendix.

If the plug runs dry, or the oil does not reach the lower line, you must refill with the oil indicated by the manufacturer.

If the oil touches or slightly exceeds the upper line, do not worry, it will eventually regulate itself.

If the oil is well above the top line, you should try to remove some of it. Doing it from the bottom of the bike can cause you to lose all the oil, so I recommend using a syringe connected to a hose.

The engine oil level is checked with the motorcycle cold if it is wet sump, and with the motorcycle warm if it is dry sump. If you do not know whether your bike is wet or dry sump, you can check it in the owner's manual.

There are motorcycles that have a sight glass (called porthole), through which you can see the oil, between two lines. If you can no longer see the oil, the oil level is too low.

✗ Oil change

This is probably the most appropriate task to get started in the mechanics and maintenance of a motorcycle.

The oil gradually loses its properties and is loaded with residues, so it must be completely replaced from time to time.

This period depends on each manufacturer (and comes in the manual of your bike), but every 3,000 mi / 5.000 km is usually a good reference.

It should be more frequent if you usually drive in the city, since the wear of the elements is greater, with a high use of the clutch and low gears.

By the way, when changing the oil always remember to change the oil filter as well.

The steps to change the oil in your motorcycle are as follows:

1) Determine what oil your motorcycle uses, not just any oil will do. You can find it in the manual of your motorcycle. It is possible that your bike uses several oils (engine, transmission, cardan). If you get to work, it is a good time to change them all.
2) Buy the oil and oil filter. It is advisable to replace it whenever the oil is changed.
3) Open the filler cap before the drain plug. It is at the top of the crankcase. If you open the drain plug and then cannot open the filler plug (because the nut is too tight, for example), you will have a big problem.
4) Place a container under the motorcycle.

5) Open the oil drain plug. This may be the same compartment as the oil filter.
6) Let the entire oil reservoir drain. It will have a dark color. The longer you have taken to change it, the darker it will be.
7) Insert the new filter and close the drain plug.
8) Fill with the amount indicated in the manual (or check the oil level).
9) Take the dirty oil to a clean point, it is very polluting.

6.5 Engine cooling

The engine, as we have learned, harbors a veritable inferno inside.

On the one hand, in the combustion chamber (whose name is already frightening), thousands of explosions are produced by the spark of the spark plug on the mixture of air and gasoline.

The piston, on the other hand, rises and falls endlessly inside the cylinder, grinding metal against metal in an endless sequence.

In addition to this, many other parts move and collide with each other without stopping, such as the rocker arms over the valves, the transmission gears or the connecting rods with the crankshaft.

It is logical to think that, in this succession of explosions, frictions and blows, very high temperatures are reached.

The engines are built with the most advanced metal alloys, however, high temperatures end up affecting the properties and geometry of all the parts involved, even more so when they are exposed to a punctual overexertion, such as an acceleration or a prolonged slope.

This is why it is absolutely necessary to cool the engine, to prevent overheating from ruining it forever.

There are basically three types of engine cooling:

1) Air cooling

It is very common to find cylinders with many steel sheets on the outside. These are fins that allow air to circulate between them, cooling the engine as it passes through. It should be remembered that an engine is designed to work while in motion, so a motorcycle that has been running for a long time without moving tends to heat up.

Picture 32.   Air-cooled engine

The fins are usually painted black to promote heat radiation away from the engine.

It is usually the system used in small engines, and in almost all two-stroke engines.

2) Water or liquid cooling

In this case, a liquid is introduced between the outside air and the engine to help dissipate engine heat.

This liquid is usually distilled water with an antifreeze (usually glycol). The additive gives the water the properties of not freezing, not boiling and not oxidizing the cooling lines.

The basis of the system is the entry of liquid at low temperature into the engine, inside which it performs a path in which it heats up as it cools the engine (the engine temperature is transferred to the coolant). At the end of its path, it is released to the outside and goes to a radiator. In this radiator, thanks to the ambient air, the liquid cools down again and starts its cycle again.

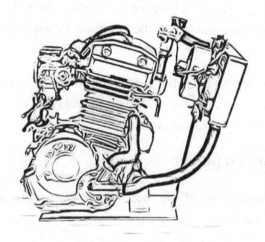

Picture 33.   Water-cooled engine

These systems usually have a thermostat, which keeps the liquid circulating inside the engine until the temperature rises and it is necessary to cool it in the radiator.

3) Oil cooling

In addition to the systems listed above, the lubricating oil is the component most responsible for the cooling of the four-stroke engine, hence its good condition and periodic replacement is vital.

The oil runs through all the internal parts of the engine, fulfilling its lubrication and cooling function, and finally falls to the bottom of the crankcase.

✖ Coolant level check

In water cooling systems, it is necessary to check that the coolant level is between the two marks on the reservoir or expansion tank. This should always be done when the engine is cold.

When performing this operation, check the condition of the radiator, in case the fins are bent, in which case, you should separate them with the help of a flat plastic tool, being very careful not to damage it.

6.6 Torque vs. power

Torque or power is one of the most heated discussions among bikers since the dawn of time.

I would have preferred not to touch on the subject because its full understanding is far from a basic mechanics book, however, I don't want you to miss a cursory idea of the difference between torque and horsepower. At least so you can win an argument with your brother-in-law.

We can all understand what strength is. If we think of someone who has a lot of strength, it is easy for us to imagine a muscular person with the ability to lift any weight.

In a motorcycle (or in any engine), any movement or demonstration of force is necessarily associated with a rotation. The piston turns the crankshaft, the crankshaft turns the gearbox, the gearbox turns a chain, belt or cardan shaft, and the latter turns a wheel.

That is, it is impossible to understand the "force" of a motorcycle without relating it to a rotation. For this reason, when we talk about an engine, we use the magnitude torque. Torque is a force associated with a rotation.

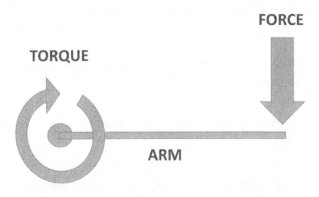

Picture 34.   Torque diagram

Logically, the force is the force made by the piston pushed by the explosion, and the torque is the rotation we get on the crankshaft.

Torque is measured in Nm (Newton for force and meters for distance).

We have already managed to turn our crankshaft, and no matter how much force our piston makes, even if we have the bike with the biggest piston in the universe and the world torque record, with that turn of the crankshaft, our bike will not have moved more than one centimeter.

This is where the concept of power comes in.

It is no use if we are able to produce a very large torque, if we do not do it many times in a row.

The power relates the engine torque to the number of revolutions we are able to give, that is to say, to the revolutions per minute (rpm).

$$Power = torque \times revolutions$$

Normally, it is valid to say that the higher the rpm, the more power we will have. This is true up to a point where friction, overheating, and the difficulty the engine has to perform its work at a very high-speed stops producing power (because the torque drops).

The most common example to explain torque and power is that of the cyclist.

- The force is the force exerted by the cyclist's leg on the pedal.
- The arm is the pedal crank.
- Torque is the force transmitted through the crank, i.e., the moment of force on the bottom bracket shell, or if you prefer, on the crankset.
- Power is the cyclist's ability to maintain that torque while pedaling without stopping. Your power will be greater if you can pedal many times in a row.

Finally, if you look at any technical data sheet, where the power is expressed (in horsepower or HP), rpm is always specified, and the same happens with the torque.

For example, the Kawasaki Vulcan S delivers 61 hp at 7,500 rpm. Maximum torque is 63 Nm at 6,600 rpm.

This is because, as we have seen, the power is the product of a torque by a number of revolutions, which is to say, it is a curve. In the data sheets they give you the highest point of the curve, which corresponds to a specific number of revolutions per minute.

74

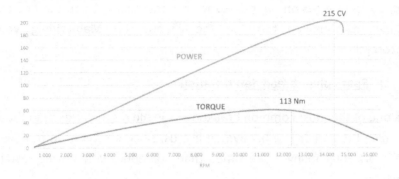

Picture 35.   Torque-power graph

You may think that the torque has nothing to do with the rpm, however, in a cylinder does not enter the same amount of mixture when we are idling, that when we give gas, therefore the explosion will not be the same, and torque either. There comes a time when the torque stops rising with rpm and begins to decrease. This happens because the cylinder cannot take advantage of all the mixture that enters it to generate more torque, due to the very high speed of the piston and the opening and closing of valves, not to mention friction and heating.

6.7   Common engine failures

Most engine failures are usually due to a lack of maintenance or an overly aggressive driving style.

They are therefore avoidable to a certain extent.

These are breakdowns that will necessarily have to be attended to in a specialized workshop and I am afraid they will not come cheap.

However, there are certain tasks that do not pose a great difficulty and that you can dare to perform, especially those related to the maintenance of external parts of the engine.

I am going to focus on the breakdowns in this chapter. You can find the engine maintenance tasks in the chapter on **Maintaining your motorcycle**.

1) Spark plug thread deterioration

It is one of the most common breakdowns in old motorcycles or in those in which the owner is a handyman like us, since he will have removed the spark plug many more times than someone with no interest in mechanics.

Tightening the spark plug too hard can damage the thread printed on the cylinder head, losing part of its sealing.

It has a relatively simple solution, by inserting a bushing that is machined with a new thread.

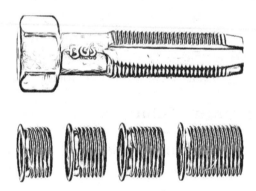

Picture 36.   Spark plug thread repair taps and bushings

Just don't overdo it next time.

2) The dreaded seizure

There's nothing scarier than a motorcycle going on the fritz.

When we subject a piston to excessive speed in the absence of sufficient lubrication, the temperature will rise to such an extent that the piston melts, or rubs against the cylinder liner without lubrication, causing major damage.

At this point the engine stops running, as the piston cannot run freely inside the cylinder. The motorcycle will quickly lose power and will not start again because of a blocked piston. This can cause the rear wheel to lock up and you could end up on the asphalt.

If you have enough reflexes to operate the clutch, you will avoid the fall.

Picture 37.   Seized piston

This is a problem of proper engine maintenance, basically not changing the oil.

It is solved by replacing all the damaged elements, and normally by rectifying the cylinder.

It is one of the most serious breakdowns on a motorcycle.

3) Piston head breakage

It is caused by overheating or by the wrong choice of spark plug, which at a temperature higher than it can withstand, breaks and falls on the piston and pierces it.

It can be caused by the collision of the piston with a valve or with any foreign body dislodged in the combustion chamber.

This failure requires the replacement of the piston. It is very serious, although it is not frequent.

Picture 38.   Piston head breakage

4) Cylinder head gasket

When the gasket that seals the cylinder head deteriorates, we will have lost the cylinder sealing, so that when the pressure increases (compression phase), mixture and oil will escape.

This problem is much more serious in liquid-cooled engines, as a leak will allow coolant to enter the combustion chamber and burn.

At that moment a very characteristic cloud of white smoke with a sweet smell will form.

5) The engine gets hot

This can be caused by numerous factors, however, since there is a system in charge of lowering the engine temperature, we will focus on analyzing whether that system is working properly.

The most drastic consequences of overheating are cylinder head gasket failure and seizure.

If the motorcycle is air-cooled there will be little to check, since, beyond the engine fins are not clogged, there is nothing else to do. In this case it is advisable to check the engine oil level, and especially its color. If it is totally black, you will have to change it.

On water-cooled motorcycles, check the coolant level (there are two marks on the expansion tank and the liquid must be between them). Also check that the radiator is in good condition and does not have flattened areas. You must also check that it is well purged.

The cause may be a faulty thermostat, which does not allow the liquid to escape to the radiator to cool down, or a clogged pump.

6) Engine is too cold

When an engine does not reach its correct operating temperature, it is due to a malfunction of the cooling system thermostat.

The function of this is to allow coolant to enter the engine when it has warmed up. If it does this prematurely (or always) the engine will run too cold.

In this case the pressure switch must be properly regulated, if it allows it, otherwise it will have to be replaced.

7) Motorcycle consumes oil

Oil is used to lubricate the engine, particularly those parts that are subject to continuous friction or high temperatures. It circulates in every nook and cranny of the engine and a certain amount of oil consumption is not a cause for concern. A consumption of between 1% and 1.5% of gasoline consumption is considered acceptable.

However, excessive consumption can be a symptom of major problems.

If you have to top up the oil frequently because the oil level is below the indicator stripes, it is likely that your bike is leaking oil (sorry!).

One of the easiest ways to detect that a bike is burning oil (because burning oil is the most likely way to lose oil) is to put your hand on the exhaust outlet when it is not too hot. If the smoke is "sticky" or smells a lot like burning, you are more than likely burning oil.

The most common causes of a motorcycle burning oil are worn piston rings or bad valve guides.

In the first case, the oil enters the combustion chamber from below, from the crankcase. The rings do not fulfill their function of keeping this chamber watertight, and part of the lubricating oil manages to enter the chamber, burning during the explosion phase. This is solved by changing the rings. Sometimes it may be necessary to rectify the cylinder.

The easiest way to measure the condition of the piston rings is by means of a compression test, in which it is measured if the compression chamber is watertight, by inserting a threaded pressure gauge in the spark plug hole and turning the engine. This is a very simple test that you should be familiar with before venturing to disassemble the piston.

If the problem is in the valves, the oil enters the combustion chamber from above. The valve seals are not able to keep the oil used for lubricating the valves in their corresponding grooves, and it ends up falling into the chamber and burning in the explosion. This is solved by repairing the valves.

If the smoke appears when accelerating, it is likely to be a valve problem. If, on the other hand, it appears when reducing, it may be a piston ring problem.

The bike can also leak oil from the crankcase. See if there is a spot on the floor where the bike sleeps. While a small drip is normal and acceptable, a puddle of oil should worry you.

8) Water at oil change

If you find water or foam when changing the oil, it is likely that there is a leak in the cooling circuit.

This leak is probably in the cylinder head or its gasket.

It is necessary to disassemble the cylinder head and locate the leak, and it is not a simple or cheap task.

9) Oil pressure light does not turn off

If the oil warning light (red and with an oilcan symbol) does not go out quickly when you start your motorcycle, stop it immediately.

It indicates that you have run out of oil and must replenish it. Otherwise, you may even damage the bike.

If after checking the oil level you find that it is correct, you probably have an electrical fault.

Either the oil pressure contact is broken (it is threaded into the crankcase and is not too expensive) or there is a bad contact.

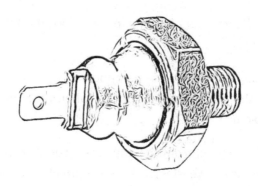

Picture 39.　　　Oil contact

7 Distribution

The timing system of an engine is responsible for opening and closing its valves.

We have seen that the intake and exhaust valves are responsible for letting the gasoline-air mixture into the cylinder and letting the explosion gases out, respectively.

We have also seen that they must be opened and closed at very specific times.

The distribution system is responsible for ensuring that the valves open and close at the right time.

Every movement in the engine has its origin in an explosion (with the exception of the first movement, which will be produced by the starter motor or by a pedal kick).

This explosion displaces the piston downward, which initiates the movement of the crankshaft. This crankshaft sets in motion a series of gears and belts that serve different purposes:

- As a main function, the rotation is used to move a chain or cardan shaft, which moves a wheel and makes our motorcycle work.
- On the other hand, the rotation is used by the alternator to generate electric current.
- That rotation is also used to start several pumps, which move oil, water or coolant throughout the engine.
- The twist will be used to get our spark plug to produce a spark at the right time.
- Finally, this rotation is used, by means of gears, chains or belts, to open and close the valves, which will give way to the mixture

that will cause the next explosion. This is precisely what distribution is all about.

As you can see, that first explosion really pays off.

Picture 40.   Distribution operation

7.1   Distribution elements

We are going to review the elements that make up the distribution system in an engine.

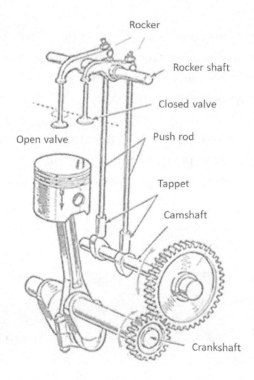

Picture 41.   Parts of the distribution system

- 🏍 **Valves**: they are the main part of the system. They are in charge of regulating the mixture inlet into the combustion chamber (intake valves) and the gases outlet from the combustion chamber (exhaust valves). As a minimum, we will have two per cylinder; one intake and one exhaust valve, but this number may vary.

In general, sport engines mount a higher number of valves, while quieter engines usually settle for two valves.

🏍 **Camshaft**: a cam is a metal part whose geometry forces another part to perform a certain movement.

Imagine a music box. It is nothing more than a cylinder with notches that, as it rotates, moves keys that compose a melody. If the cylinder turns faster, the melody will sound faster, but it will always be the same melody.

The same thing happens with the camshaft, the speed can vary, but for a given radius of rotation of the shaft containing the cams, the valves will be in a specific opening position.

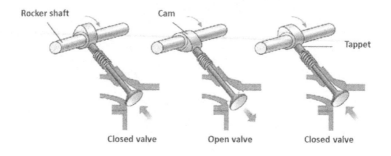

Picture 42.   Cam movement

The camshaft is the piece that organizes all the cams, to open and close the valves in a coordinated way. To me it reminds me of the wooden crosshead that controls a puppet as with a single piece you can move both arms and legs.

A single camshaft can drive all valves, or several camshafts can be installed so that each camshaft drives a group of valves, this option being the one adopted by sports engines.

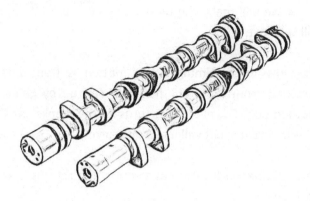

Picture 43.   Camshaft

🏍 **Rocker arm**: it is a metal part similar to a seesaw, hence its name. It is responsible for transmitting the thrust from the pusher (coming from the cam) to the valve. Rocker arms rotate around the rocker arm shaft.

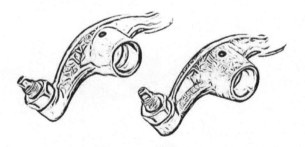

Picture 44.   Rocker arms

🏍 **Pusher or push rod**: it is in charge of transmitting the movement from the cam to the rocker arm, or directly to the valve. The cylinder that performs the thrust is called tappet.

🏍 **Adjusting screw and nut**: screw that allows to regulate the opening degree of a valve for a specific cam position. What we really do is to lengthen or shorten the pusher. By means of this screw we will make the tappet or valve adjustment, which we will see next.

- **Transmission or timing drive**: motion is transmitted to the camshaft from the crankshaft and can be by gears, chain or toothed belt. For every two turns of the crankshaft (1 cylinder cycle), the camshaft will make one turn.

- **Valve spring**: each valve has a spring that returns it to its closed position.

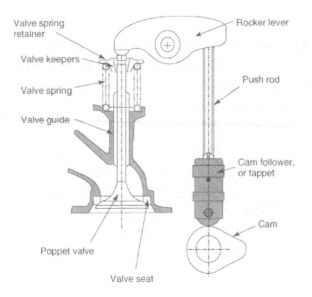

Picture 45.   Schematic diagram of valve opening

- **Seat**: part on which the valve sits to close. It is like the door frame. They are made of very resistant materials as they have to withstand continuous knocking.

> *In the past, lead from gasoline was used as a lubricant for valve seats and valve guides. Its disappearance forced them to be reinforced.*
>
> *On classic motorcycles it is necessary to add a lead additive to the gasoline.*

- 🏍 **Guides**: ducts through which the valves slide, to avoid damaging the cylinder heads.

7.2 Types of distribution

Camshafts are usually located in the cylinder head so that they are as close as possible to the valves to avoid remote transmissions.

However, in the past (and therefore it is still easy to find them on motorcycles of a few years ago), the camshafts were located in the crankcase, close to the crankshaft, which made it necessary to use long rods or belts to transmit the movement of the cams.

Depending on the location of the camshaft and the way in which the power is applied to the valves, different types of valve timing are distinguished, which often give their name to the engine type itself:

- 🏍 **OHV** (Over Head Valve): overhead camshaft.
- 🏍 **OHC** (Over Head Cam): overhead camshaft.
- 🏍 **DOHC** (Double Over Head Cam): double overhead camshaft.

Although mentioned above, it is worth remembering that a valve can be actuated by a rocker arm, by a pusher, or directly by the cam. There will always be a cam, but between the cam and the valve there may (or may not) be other elements such as pushers and rocker arms.

There are advanced timing systems, which allow to vary the valve opening speed depending on the number of revolutions, so that, at higher revolutions, the valve opening is greater. Their detailed explanation is beyond the scope of this basic manual.

7.3 Distribution regulation

As explained above, the explosion inside the combustion chamber generates a chain of events that leads, after passing through numerous elements, to the opening and closing of the valves.

It is easy to deduce that this opening or closing cannot take place at any given moment, but that everything must be totally synchronized, as if it were an orchestra.

The intake valves must open at a specific moment (and for milliseconds) for the mixture to enter the cylinder and close just a moment later.

The same will happen with the exhaust valves, which will have a unique moment in time to open and let the combustion gases escape and must close a few thousandths of a second later.

If all this were not perfectly regulated, it would be a real disaster. The best thing that can happen to a motorcycle in that case is that it won't start.

You will not have to deal with a timing adjustment, unless you disassemble the engine of your motorcycle, a task that is far from a basic mechanics manual. It will be up to the manufacturer to do it perfectly.

In geared systems, where each gear can occupy as many positions as it has teeth, it is usual for the manufacturer to include reference points to know how these gears should be positioned, guaranteeing a correct distribution setting.

The first time I opened an engine, without having any knowledge of mechanics at the time, it was that of a Ducati Forza 350 that I had named "Lucky".

I did it out of sheer curiosity, to find out what was hidden inside. After carefully reassembling everything, the bike did not start for days. I left my leg on the starter pedal of a bike that, to make matters worse, has enormous compression.

I didn't realize my mistake until I opened the engine again: on the gears that I had so carefully assembled, there were four little dots that had to match. Obviously, they didn't, it would have been too much of a coincidence. As soon as I aligned them, the bike started the first time.

Picture 46.   "Lucky" gears, fretworked

7.4   Valve adjustment or tappet adjustment

There is one task that we can do ourselves. This is valve adjustment.

By the way, this is only valid for a 4-stroke engine. Don't look for the valves in a 2-stroke engine, because you won't find them.

As seen above, the valves are responsible for letting the mixture of air and gasoline into the cylinder, and for letting the gases produced during combustion out.

It must be understood that, in such a measured process, the doors must be totally hermetic and not only that, but they must also open and close perfectly. We cannot forget that these are metal doors subjected to a high temperature, and that, therefore, they will expand in a normal operating regime. This means that, when cold, there must be clearances which, when the valves are heated, will close.

It is precisely this clearance that we adjust when adjusting the valves and, therefore, it **must always be done when the** engine **is cold.**

What happens if the valves are not properly adjusted?

If the valve clearance is not properly adjusted, two situations can occur:

1. If there is too much clearance, the valve will not close completely until it is very hot. This causes an annoying knocking or rattling and results in a poor use of the force of the explosions (we do not get the absolute tightness of the combustion chamber and the gases escape).

2. If there is too little clearance, when the motorcycle is hot, the valves will remain closed (valves stuck), so the mixture will not enter the cylinder properly, nor will all the combustion gases be able to escape.

How often should the valves be adjusted?

There is no single answer to this question, as it depends on the bike and your riding style.

It is usually recommended to do it every 15,000 mi / 25.000 km, however, if you have problems with starting or response of the bike, or if you notice a big difference between cold and hot operation, it may be a good time to do it.

✖ How to adjust the valves?

Before making the adjustment, be sure to get a set of feeler gauges. These are thin sheets of metal whose thickness is known in advance. They allow us to accurately adjust the clearance.

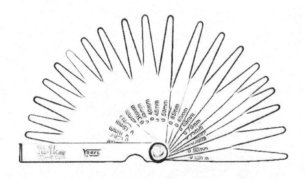

Picture 47.   Thickness gauges

To start adjusting the valves, we will have to lift the valve cover (usually found on the cylinder head) to expose the valves and remove the spark plugs (to work without compression).

In addition, we must make sure that the piston is at its TDC (Top Dead Center) which follows the compression stroke.

To do this we will move the crankshaft using the screw that protrudes from the crankshaft to perform this type of task. Each motorcycle has this adjustment screw at a different point, so you should look for it in the documentation.

It is easy to locate this position, because the valves will be "loose", otherwise, in any other position, the valves will be "stepped" and will have no clearance at all. If you grab them with your hand, you will notice that they move slightly.

If you have no way to turn the crankshaft, you can slightly move the rear wheel of your bike with a gear engaged.

Most motorcycles have signals that tell you the position of the piston at any given time. Get your motorcycle's workshop manual (if it is not in the owner's manual) and locate these signals for optimal results.

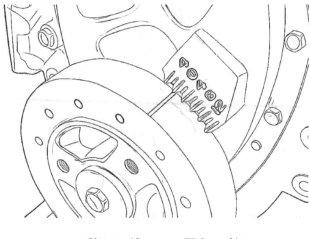

Picture 48.   TDC marking

Finally, get the manufacturer's recommended clearances for your bike. This is different for each model and appears in the bike's manual.

Intake valve clearance is usually different from exhaust valve clearance.

You are now ready to start.

Remember that, after the valve adjustment, the rocker arm covers gaskets must be replaced to ensure proper sealing.

There are several systems for regulating the valves, which I will summarize below.

a) Nut-screw system:

It is common to find them in distributions with rocker arms. In this case, a more or less tightened screw is the one that marks the clearance of the valve, which will be operated by means of a rocker arm.

To set the desired clearance, always with the engine cold, we will introduce between the screw and the rocker arm the gauge corresponding to the clearance set by the manufacturer of our motorcycle.

Loosen the nut and tighten or loosen the screw until it touches the gauge. It is important that the gauge comes out without forcing it. It is useless to crush the gauge with the screw and deform it.

It may be the case that there is no rocker arm, or that the screw is in the rocker arm head itself. The procedure is the same, look for the bolt, and adjust the clearance with a feeler gauge.

The clearance measurements are less than one millimeter, so we use gauges, which are thin metal sheets of the desired size.

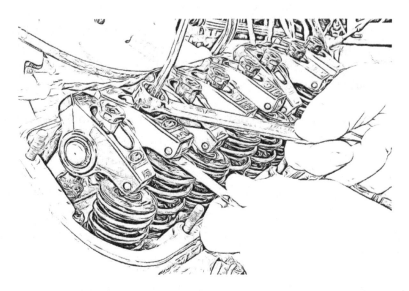

Picture 49.   Valve adjustment with nut and bolt

b) Systems with calibrated pickup

This system is the most commonly used on modern motorcycles.

It has a millimetrically calibrated pad, which we will have to replace with another one in case we want to modify the clearance between cams and valves.

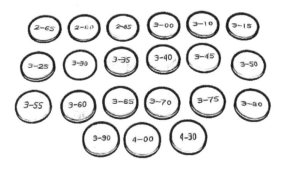

Picture 50.   Calibrated pads

This requires disassembling the entire camshaft, which I do not recommend if you are not an expert mechanic.

c) Hydraulic self-regulating systems

On certain high-end motorcycles, you will never have to worry about adjusting their valves, as they have a hydraulic system that always maintains the necessary clearance.

7.5 Typical distribution system breakdowns

Distribution failures are not usually within the reach of a novice mechanic.

Apart from the valve adjustment already explained, other breakdowns require the disassembly of numerous internal engine components, which I do not recommend unless you know what you are doing.

We will review the most frequent malfunctions, especially in order to know how to recognize them when they occur.

1) Chain or timing belt breakage

This malfunction is neither easy nor inexpensive to fix.

Before waiting for a chain to break, taking everything in its path, it is recommended that every time the engine is opened for maintenance, the elongation of the timing chain be measured. That is, how much it has stretched from its original size.

For this purpose, the manufacturers indicate the dimension that must exist between two specific points of the chain. If this dimension is greater than the permissible one, the entire chain must be replaced.

The chain lasts longer than the belt.

There are many signs that the belt or chain is starting to fail. The problem is that they can be confused with other faults.

These include a lack of response when accelerating, difficulty starting the bike (both can be mistaken for problems in the power supply or valve timing), finding metal shavings in the oil change (if you have a belt they will come from somewhere else), or a metallic rattle at idle (this may be due to poor valve timing).

2) Belt tensioner in bad condition

It is rare for a chain to break. You must have neglected a lot of maintenance.

However, it is very common for the element in charge of keeping the belt taut to break down: the belt tensioner.

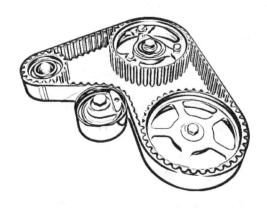

Picture 51.   Belt tensioner

As with any spring-driven element, springs can lose their capacity and must be replaced when they no longer adequately tension the belt.

3) Valve burnout

Due to incorrect or non-existent valve adjustment, the valve clearance may be too small. This causes the valve to be "stuck" when hot and does not close its cavity. As it is not completely closed, when the explosion occurs, it affects areas of the valve that are not prepared for it, thus deteriorating it.

When a valve has burned out, it is necessary to replace it, with all its elements.

It is solved with a regular valve adjustment. Every 15,000 mi / 25.000 km is a suitable frequency.

8 Transmission

The engine, by moving the piston, is able to generate a movement that will be useless if we do not manage to transfer it to the wheels.

Transferring that motion from the piston to the wheels is the function of the transmission.

Within the transmission system we have to talk about four elements:

a) The <u>primary transmission</u>: connects the crankshaft to the clutch.
b) The <u>clutch</u>: the element that allows us to change gears
c) The gearbox
d) <u>Secondary transmission</u>: chain, belt or cardan shaft

8.1 Primary transmission

The function of the primary transmission is to connect the crankshaft to the clutch.

In essence it is a shaft with a larger gear than the crankshaft gear, i.e., designed to reduce the rotational speed with respect to the crankshaft. It is often a large ring gear attached to the clutch at the rear.

It can be connected to it by sprockets (straight or helical) or by chain.

At the end of this shaft, we will find a large cylindrical piece that rotates in a solid manner. This is the clutch.

Picture 52.   Primary transmission

8.2   The clutch

The piston goes up and down all the time, faster or slower, but as long as the bike is started, it will never stop.

Even if we are waiting at a traffic light. The piston goes up and down.

When you brake, the piston moves up and down.

On the other hand, at this point in the book I imagine you already know that a motorcycle has different gears, in essence larger gears and smaller gears, but how do you change gears if the engine never stops spinning? If we tried to change gears with the engine spinning at 5,000 rpm, the gears would blow up.

That's what the clutch is for.

The clutch is nothing more than a mechanism capable of rotating at one end (always, since the engine side never stops) and making the other end (the end where the gearbox is) sometimes rotate and other times be stationary.

Let's see it with a very illustrative example: a blender making mayonnaise.

Imagine the blender. It has a propeller that never stops, it is always turning. It is the engine.

On the other hand, we have the glass in which we will make the mayonnaise. When the mayonnaise is liquid, the glass will be stationary. No matter how much the blender propeller turns, we can leave the glass loose and it will not move. The glass is the gearbox.

At a given moment, the mayonnaise will emulsify, it will become a paste capable of dragging the glass with the movement of the propeller. At that moment, if we do not hold the glass, it will be able to rotate to the rhythm of the mixer.

The mayonnaise is the clutch in our example. It is able to keep the beaker stationary even though the mixer is spinning at full speed, and at the moment (when emulsifying) it is able to drag the beaker to the rhythm of the propeller.

Clutch operation

Having understood the clutch fundamentals, we will now explain how it works.

The clutch is composed of different alternating discs. Half of them are called friction discs and are made of a rough material, capable of dragging the rest.

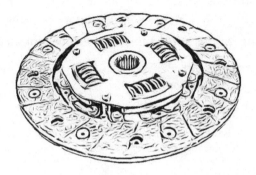

Picture 53.   Friction disc

The other half is made of metal. The metal discs (clutch plates) alternate with the drag discs.

Each type of disc moves to the beat of a shaft. The shaft coming from the crankshaft will move one type of disc and the shaft going to the gearbox will move the opposite type of disc.

That is, if the crankshaft moves the drive discs, then the gearbox will move the metal discs. If, on the other hand, the crankshaft moves the metal discs, then the drive discs will move with the gear shaft. This will depend on the clutch design.

The important thing to understand is that each group of discs moves on a different axis.

- Shaft coming from the crankshaft: moves one type of disc.
- Shaft that exits to the gears: moves a different type of disc.

With the clutch relaxed, without actuating the lever, powerful springs are responsible for holding the metal discs together with the brake discs. In this way, the friction discs are able to "drag" the metal discs, causing the whole assembly to rotate when the crankshaft is turning.

Since the friction discs rotate in conjunction with the gear shaft, the gear shaft moves at the pace set by the primary transmission. In other words, everything rotates at the same rate as the crankshaft rotates.

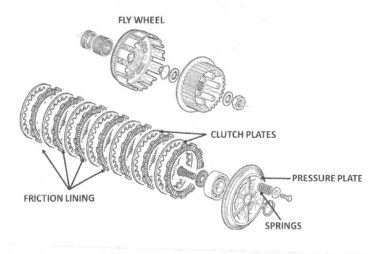

Picture 54.   Multi plate Clutch parts

When we squeeze the clutch lever, what we are doing is transmitting a force to a pusher, capable of overcoming the force of the clutch springs and separating the metal discs from the brake discs.

At this moment, as the friction discs do not rub hard enough against the metallic ones, the friction discs, which are the ones that rotate with the gear shaft, can stop to allow a gear to be engaged. The metallic ones never stop rotating, since they do it with the crankshaft.

The clutch is "engaged" when the lever is pressed, and "disengaged" at rest.

Unpacked	Handle tightened	Clutch shaft and shift shaft loose
Clutching	Handle at rest	Clutch shaft and shift shaft joined together

Clutch types

There are several types of clutches, depending on the number of discs or their lubrication:

- 🏍 By number of disks:

    o **Monodisc**: if we only have one driving disc and one metal disc
    o **Multi plate**: if we have several disks of each type

Picture 55.   Multidisc clutch

- 🏍 For its lubrication

    o **Dry**: if not submerged in oil
    o **In oil bath**: if immersed in oil

The automatic transmission of a scooter

If you've ever ridden a scooter, you'll have noticed that you don't need to clutch or shift gears.

This is because they are automatic scooters, i.e., their clutch adapts the shift to the speed of the motorcycle automatically. This makes scooters very comfortable and easy to ride.

This type of motorcycle is equipped with a centrifugal shoe clutch.

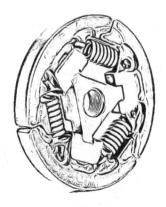

Picture 56.   Centrifugal clutch

In this case, the part with the ability to "drag" is formed by pads, called clutch pads, composed of a rough material.

These pads (usually 3) are arranged on the outside of a plate that rotates thanks to the belt coming from the crankshaft.

When the crankshaft (or, in other words, the engine) rotates slowly, at idle speed, the centrifugal force cannot separate the pads from the plate, and the rear wheel of the motorcycle remains stationary (e.g., when the motorcycle is started, stopped at a traffic light).

When we accelerate, the centrifugal force increases, separating the pads from the plate. At that moment, they enter into friction with the outer disc, which is the one that transmits the movement to the rear wheel.

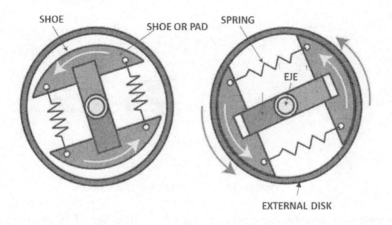

Picture 57.   Operation of a centrifugal clutch

In addition to the centrifugal clutch, scooters also have a different gear-shifting system, very similar to that of a bicycle. Its key part is the **variator**, which also works thanks to centrifugal force.

In this case it is a double bell that rotates with the crankshaft shaft and closes as the speed increases (thanks to rollers that move towards the outside of the bell due to centrifugal force).

When riding at low speed, the bells are separated, so the belt is at the lowest point of the junction of the two parts (comparable to the small chainring on a bicycle). As we accelerate, the bells come together, forcing the belt to run at a higher point in the "valley" between the two parts (comparable to the large chainring on a bicycle).

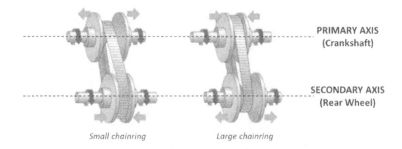

PRIMARY AXIS
(Crankshaft)

SECONDARY AXIS
(Rear Wheel)

Small chainring   *Large chainring*

Picture 58.   Variator of a scooter

The belt of a scooter supports an important number of tensions in its operation, which is why it is convenient not to lose sight of the recommended periods for its change, since it can leave us stranded at any time if it breaks. This period ranges from 7,000 to 10,000 mi (12.000 to 17.000 km). The belt will send us signals that it is beginning to end its useful life when we notice that the motorcycle does not reach its original speeds.

8.3   The gearbox

The clutch is the element that allows the gear change to be carried out smoothly, otherwise, exchanging gears that rotate at thousands of revolutions per minute would be an impossible and dangerous task.

For the explanation of the gearbox, we will once again use a well-known example: the gearbox of a bicycle.

Nowadays, *fixie bikes* are very fashionable, or fixed gear bikes, that is, with only one gear, however, imagine that with that same bike you want to do a sprint or climb a mountain. Unless you have legs of steel, you're going to have a hard time.

That is why gears exist, to adapt the engine power to each situation.

- When the wheel feed presents a great difficulty, for example, due to a steep slope, you will need a **higher torque**, even if it is at the cost of reducing the speed. In other words, you need a lower gear. This will also be the case when coming out of a stop, where you have to overcome the friction of the wheel on the ground.
- However, when you are already riding at a good speed on a flat or downhill, you have no significant forces to overcome, and you want a higher speed. In this situation, you give up torque for speed, i.e., you need a high gear.

When the gear is not adequate for the force to be overcome, whether it is a steep hill or simply when coming out of a STOP, the torque will be insufficient, and your bike will stall.

Motorcycles can have a wide variety of gears, although 5 gears are the most common.

It is also common that the gearshift is on the left foot, that the first gear is engaged by pressing down and the rest of the gears by pressing up with the toe. Neutral will be found between first and second gear (although there will always be more).

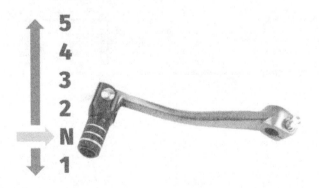

Picture 59.   Motorcycle gear diagram

How does a motorcycle gearbox work?

Going back to the bicycle simile, in essence, the gearing of a motorcycle is made up of two axles (in the bicycle it would be the bottom bracket axle and the rear wheel axle) with different gears of different sizes (in the bicycle we also have gears of different sizes, in the chainrings and in the sprockets).

The first gear, which provides the most torque, and therefore the least speed (I remind you that the formula is power=torque*speed). Just like on a bike, it will consist of a small gear on the first shaft, called the primary gear shaft, and a large gear on the secondary shaft (small chainring - large sprocket).

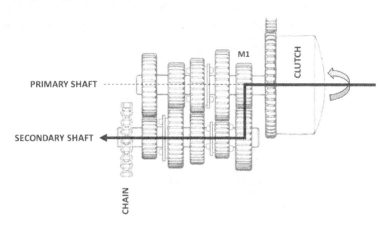

Picture 60.   First gear

The last or longest gear will be the opposite, a large gear on the primary shaft and a small gear on the secondary shaft (large chainring - small sprocket).

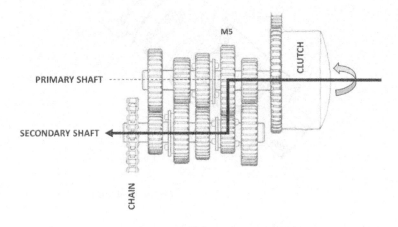

Picture 61.   Last gear

The intermediate gears will be formed by combinations also intermediate between these extremes.

The ratio of the number of teeth in the secondary gear to the number of teeth in the primary gear is called the **gear ratio**. The gear ratio will be high in low gears and low (below 1) in high gears.

To change from one gear combination to another we will use the shift pedal, which moves a part called the selector, in charge of moving the gears.

Picture 62.   Change selector

There are three types of sprockets inside the gearbox:

- 🛵 **Sliding sprockets**: rotate with their shaft and can also slide longitudinally across it.
- 🛵 **Idler sprockets**: they do not rotate with the axis on which they are located, but with the opposite axis when engaged. They do not move longitudinally along their axis.
- 🛵 **Fixed sprockets**: they rotate with their shaft and cannot move across it. There are usually two of them and they are on the primary shaft.

The basis of gear shifting is to move the sliding pinions until they are in contact with an idler (by means of steel cylinders or lugs). When this happens, the idler that was rotating with the opposite shaft is able to move its own shaft as well, and the gear is engaged or "engaged".

The gear selector, which we move with our left foot, is in charge of moving the sliding sprockets to engage the gears.

8.4 Secondary transmission

It is in charge (finally) of transmitting the movement coming out of the gearbox to the rear wheel.

In the old days there were some vehicles, halfway between the bicycle and the moped, which had an engine that geared directly with the front wheel, being one of the few front-wheel drive "motorcycles". They were the mythical VéloSoleX.

Picture 63.   VéloSoleX

The gear that sends the motion to the wheel belongs to the secondary drive shaft and is called the **drive pinion.**

The most common secondary transmission is the chain. In addition, we will study the belt (very similar to the chain) and the cardan shaft.

Chain drive

The transmission of the movement from the secondary gear shaft to the wheel is usually by means of a steel chain.

The chain links mesh on a sprocket that rotates with the gear shaft (attack sprocket) and the rear wheel sprocket.

This joint connects two shafts that rotate in parallel: the gear shaft and the wheel shaft.

As it is a flexible joint, it allows the wheel to move freely with the suspension.

Chain maintenance is one of the most important and frequently performed maintenance tasks on a motorcycle.

*Some chains have a removable link, called a **quick link**, which allows the chain to be opened for easy removal and maintenance.*

Picture 64.   Quick link

Belt drive

The basis of the belt drive is the same as that of the chain, however, instead of using a metallic element, we will use one composed of different materials. Specifically, with a core of steel and fibers and a neoprene coating.

Belts do not need to be greased or tensioned, so they require much less maintenance than chains.

Cardan shaft drive

Imagine you have two rotating shafts, you want one of them to move the other, however, they are not aligned. To connect the two shafts, the cardan joint was invented, a mechanism that rotates on itself as it rotates.

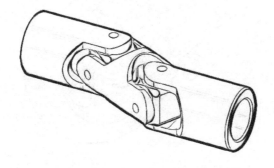

Picture 65.   Cardan joint

To give you an idea, it is the type of joint that was used on the old windsurfing boards, to hold the mast. It had to be able to rotate on itself to catch the wind, but it could also oscillate on the board, even fall on it when the surfer fell into the water.

The rotational movement of the cardan shaft transmits the rotation of the crankshaft, while the oscillating movement allows the operation of the rear transmission.

The cardan transmission, unlike the chain, is of the rigid type.

If the secondary axis of the gearbox is perpendicular to the wheel axis (i.e. the axis is longitudinal to the motorcycle), the movement will be transmitted by a bevel gear. If both axles are parallel, two bevel gears will be required, one at the output of the shift shaft, and one on the rear wheel.

The cardan shaft transmission needs much less maintenance than the chain, as it is internal, however, we must not neglect its lubrication, or changing it will be infinitely more expensive than a chain.

This is common in brands such as BMW.

Picture 66.   Cardan shaft transmission in a motorcycle

8.5 Common transmission malfunctions

The most common transmission failures are related to a lack of maintenance of the chain or a lack of lubrication of the gearbox or clutch.

Clutch failures are expensive to repair, not only because of the price of the components, but also because disassembly requires a large number of workshop hours.

1) Grease and tension the chain ⚒

The chain is a steel component that works permanently outdoors, exposed to rain, mud, frost, humidity... Not to mention the continuous pulls to which we subject it when driving.

For these reasons it must be continuously well lubricated. For this purpose, it should be cleaned (e.g. with gasoline) and greased with a rag soaked in a viscous transmission oil. You can also grease it with a chain spray.

A broken chain in motion can be very dangerous if it catches on the rear wheel.

The chain should be tensioned and greased every 300 mi / 500 km.

2) Chain slack ⚒

Excessive slack in the chain of your motorcycle is one of the most common symptoms that indicate that you should consider changing the chain.

The motorcycle's owner's manual will indicate the maximum admissible chain slack at its midpoint (with respect to the line joining the highest points of the sprocket and the attack sprocket).

For this purpose, motorcycles have chain tensioners on their swingarm. They are nothing more than pieces with screws that allow us to move the rear wheel back a few centimeters until the chain is taut. To do this we simply have to loosen the axle of the rear wheel and tighten the screws of the tensioners.

However, there comes a time when the chain has become excessively worn and must be replaced.

When changing a chain, it is advisable to change the entire drive kit, i.e. chain, sprocket and drive sprocket.

Chain manufacturers set elongation tolerances. In essence, they tell you at what limit distance between a known number of links you should change the chain.

3) Sharp teeth on the crown

The crown gear wears out before the drive sprocket. If you notice that the teeth are very sharp you should consider changing the sprocket kit soon.

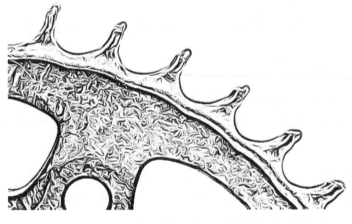

Picture 67.   Worn crown

Sharp teeth and excessive slack in the chain mean that the chain is likely to jump.

It is recommended to change the entire sprocket kit every 12,000 – 20,000 mi (20.000 – 30.000 km).

4) Chain or belt breakage

Poor maintenance of the chain or belt (or failure to change them when necessary) can cause them to break.

This will occur when the motorcycle is in motion, probably when accelerating sharply or coming out of a stop.

It is a very unpleasant breakdown that immobilizes the motorcycle and will force us to call a tow truck.

5) Clutch failure

As mentioned, clutch failures are expensive and difficult to resolve.

They are usually caused by the wear and tear of their elements (think that they spend the day rubbing against each other).

The most common is the wear of the brake discs, which must be replaced from time to time.

The springs and the pusher are also parts that tend to lose their effectiveness over time.

A poorly lubricated clutch will cause it to overheat, resulting in premature wear.

You will notice a clutch failure when you have a hard time engaging some gears, even in neutral.

You will also notice it when a gear "slips", i.e., even if you accelerate the bike will not respond as it should, losing traction.

6) Clutch cable breakage

If your bike is modern you are probably lucky enough to have a hydraulic clutch system.

However, if your bike is a few years old, your right lever will be subjected to continuous tightening, with the consequent stretching of the clutch cable. It is not in vain that it is the most frequently broken cable on the bike.

When this happens you will not be able to change gears, however, it is simple to change. Just get a new one and place it between the right lever and the clutch pusher.

7) Gearbox gear breakage

I can think of few breakdowns as serious as a gearbox gear breaking.

Gearboxes are lubricated with highly viscous oils that ensure smooth gear friction.

Running out of oil in the gearbox can cause a gear to break.

Most commonly, the broken part comes from another part of the engine (pistons, skirts, rings, etc.) that fall on the transmission, causing a major failure.

For this reason the oil plugs are magnetized, to collect any metal residue that may damage other parts.

There is no other solution than to take the bike to the workshop and have it cut open to replace the broken gear.

9 Carburetor and Injectors

We have talked at length about the engine and everything that happens inside it and we cannot forget that, for all this to happen, it is necessary to "feed" it.

The **fuel system** is responsible for introducing the mixture (in the right proportion) of air and gasoline into the cylinder.

Years ago, the most common component to fulfill this function was the carburetor but, in the most modern motorcycles (almost all those sold today), injectors are used to fulfill the same function.

9.1 The mixture of air and gasoline

Gasoline, by itself, cannot explode. It needs the presence of air to do so, that is why we will always speak of the "mixture".

You have probably heard it said that a mixture is either rich or poor. Personally, it happens to me as with one lime and one sand, I never know which is the good one.

I clarify:

- 🏍 A mixture is **rich** when it has more gasoline than necessary (it tends to be accepted that this is the case when there is less than 14.9 kg of air per kg of gasoline). This means that not all the gasoline is burned and also increases the consumption and the pollution of the motorcycle. Your spark plugs will come out black.
- 🏍 A mixture is **lean** when it has less gasoline than it should. This type of mixture overheats the engines and raises the pressure inside the engine.
- 🏍 When the mixture is perfect, i.e., both products are totally consumed, we speak of **stoichiometric mixing.**

As a consequence, there must be a system in charge of ensuring that the mixture of air and gasoline is perfect (14.9 kg of air for each kg of gasoline). This system is none other than the fuel system, and its two main components are the carburetor and the injectors.

Leaded or unleaded gasoline

In the old days, gasoline was not like what we use today. When we got to the gas station we would ask for "85 octane", "Super" or "Unleaded".

Octane ratings are a measure of the quality of gasoline against self-ignition, i.e. they measure the resistance of the temperature to explode on its own (without spark) when certain pressure and temperature levels are reached. If the octane rating were too low, it would be common for the gasoline to explode on its own before the spark ignited, causing major engine damage.

Going back to the old gasolines, these contained lead, which was gradually eliminated due to its toxic nature. Lead functioned as a lubricant for the cylinder valve seat, so these seats were reinforced with new, more resistant steel alloys.

For older motorcycles, there are lead additives that must be added to the gasoline, otherwise, excessive wear of the valve seat will occur, which will undoubtedly affect the sealing and compression of the engine.

9.2   The carburetor

As we have said, the carburetor is in charge of feeding the engine with a very precise mixture of air and gasoline, but it does not do it by its own will. It is the cylinder that sucks in the mixture.

Indeed, in its intake phase, the cylinder acts like a syringe that sucks in through the only door it has open: the intake valve.

There, at the gates of this intake valve, is the carburetor, which literally puts a surface of gasoline on a platter.

The air sucked in by the piston in its downward movement drags this gasoline, and introduces it into the cylinder.

It is important to emphasize the aspirated operation of the carburetor, as opposed to injection, which "forcibly" introduces the dosed quantity of air and gasoline.

How does a carburetor work?

In any mechanical treatise you read, they will explain that the foundation of a carburetor is based on the Venturi Principle. And so it is, but I wouldn't want to waste your attention with an overly theoretical explanation.

In essence, Venturi states that as air velocity increases, it has the ability to suck in (forgive me, physics professors).

It can be easily seen in the ground effect of Formula 1 cars, which remain stuck to the ground because of the speed of the air under them. It can also be seen in airbrushes (if you have already been encouraged to paint your bike you will know this) which, connected to an air compressor, when the air passes through the paint tank, it is able to drag the paint towards the nozzle.

The same thing happens in the carburetor, the air increases its speed inside the carburetor and is able to drag with it the gasoline requested by the cylinder.

Carburetor parts

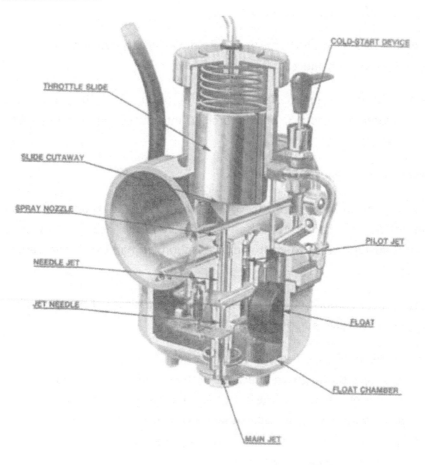

THROTTLE SLIDE

COLD-START DEVICE

SLIDE CUTAWAY

SPRAY NOZZLE

PILOT JET

NEEDLE JET

JET NEEDLE

FLOAT

FLOAT CHAMBER

MAIN JET

Picture 68.   Carburetor parts

1) **Float chamber**: is the tank where the gasoline coming from the fuel tank is stored.
2) **Pipe**: a special plastic tube for hydrocarbons that connects the fuel tank to the carburetor bowl.
3) **Float**: the fuel tank is above the carburetor so that the fuel is transported by gravity. If there were no automatic closing system, the gasoline would end up spilling out. For this purpose, there is a float inside the tank, like the one in the toilet cisterns.

When the gasoline reaches its level, the buoy (which floats) rises and closes the gasoline flow.

4) **Jets**: these are the tubes that are submerged in the gasoline to allow air to carry it away. In essence, they work like straws inside a glass. The glass would be the tank, the soda would be the gasoline, and the mouth sucking would be the cylinder asking for gasoline.

5) **Throttle slide**: the carburetor is controlled from the throttle grip. More throttle, more air in, more gasoline out. Less throttle, less air, less fuel. This is achieved with a sliding valve called the throttle slide. When we "give gas" by turning the fist, we are pulling a cable, which in turn raises the valve, letting more air in. This valve can also be a butterfly valve, in which case, by turning the throttle, we are opening a circular damper.

6) **Needle**: in addition to regulating the amount of incoming air, the hood is able to regulate the fuel intake. It achieves this thanks to a needle-shaped appendage at the bottom, which penetrates a duct as the hood is lowered. The more it penetrates into the duct (which is called the chimney or high nozzle), the more it closes it, thus shutting off the gasoline that rises through it.

7) **Membrane**: there are carburetors that are not driven by a bell, but the cylinder itself, by "sucking" air, creates a vacuum capable of driving the carburetor. These are called constant vacuum or membrane carburetors. The membrane and its spring are in charge of opening and closing the air passage when the vacuum is produced.

Idle, main and starter circuits

The operation that we have explained for the carburetor corresponds to a situation of normal operation of the motorcycle, so while we are riding. This is what is known as the **main circuit**. It is the one we control from the throttle.

125

However, when the bike is idling, or we are downshifting, we are not operating the throttle, and yet the mixture enters the cylinder, otherwise it would stop instantly.

This is due to the **idle circuit**, the mechanism in charge of supplying mixture to the engine when we are not accelerating.

Its operation is very similar. In this case the hood is lowered, and the needle completely obstructs the chimney or high nozzle, so that, a priori, no air can pass or gasoline can come up from the tank.

However, carburetors have much smaller ducts, in the direction of the air intake, through which a small amount of air penetrates, which is capable of dragging a small amount of gasoline, enough to keep the engine at idle speed.

In this case it is not the chimney that provides the gasoline, but the downstream jet.

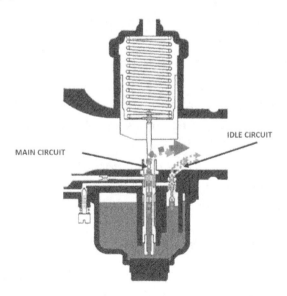

Picture 69.   Carburetor circuits

The last circuit we will explain is the **starter circuit** (or cold-start circuit). This is a mechanism for starting the motorcycle when cold, since, at low temperatures, the gasoline condenses in the carburetor ducts, and it is more difficult for the air to carry it away.

For this purpose, by means of different mechanisms, the air passage is limited (sometimes it can be called "choke", since that is precisely what it does), thus allowing the cylinder to suck in a greater amount of gasoline.

Other systems are based on increasing the fuel provided when cold, keeping the air constant.

Carburetor regulation 🔧

Carburetors allow regulating the amount of mixture entering the engine, both at high and low speed.

It does so by means of screws which, depending on their degree of tightening, open or close a duct and allow more or less air or gasoline to pass through.

The idle speed of the motorcycle (when we are not accelerating) is regulated by the **idle speed screw**. This is a screw with a conical tip which, when tightened, raises the level of the carburetor needle. Raising the needle keeps the chimney or high nozzle more open, so that the mixture will be richer in gasoline. You will find it in the middle plane of the carburetor.

Each motorcycle has its specific idle speed setting, which is expressed in the manual by a number of turns from its tightest position (loosening it).

If you do not have the data, you can adjust it when the bike is hot, loosening the screw until you notice that it is about to stall.

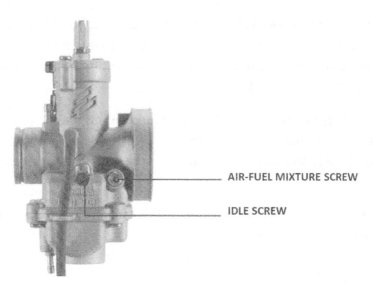

AIR-FUEL MIXTURE SCREW

IDLE SCREW

Picture 70.   Carburetor adjustment screws

When adjusting the **air fuel mixture screw** you must take into account that, depending on the carburetor model, there are screws that close air ducts and others that close gasoline ducts.

A screw that regulates an air duct, the tighter it is, will produce a richer mixture (more revolutions).

However, a screw that regulates a fuel line, the tighter it is, will produce a leaner mixture (less revolutions). This depends on the carburetor manufacturer, so I recommend that you test with the bike running.

If, when tightening the screw, the motorcycle "falls down" we will be throttling a fuel line. If, on the other hand, when tightening the screw, the motorcycle turns up, the screw throttles an air duct.

You will find this screw on the side of the carburetor, even under the carburetor.

9.3 Injection

Although we are fascinated by carburetors, the truth is that it is a system destined to disappear.

Currently, all cars are manufactured with injectors, as well as all high-performance motorcycles, with carburetors being reduced to low-displacement motorcycles and scooters.

Injection is nothing more than the application of advanced electronics to the power supply of an engine.

In this case there is no need for a complex Venturi system of ducts and air depressions. A control unit sends the precise mixture dosing orders according to the needs of the engine at any given moment.

With the use of injectors, we obtain a series of advantages:

- **Accurate mixture dosing**: the machines do not usually make mistakes. The control unit is programmed so that, when the engine is in a given situation, the amount of gasoline sprayed is a fixed amount.
- **Reduced consumption**: by adjusting the fuel quantities to the maximum precision, unnecessary consumption is reduced.
- **Engine "choking" is avoided**: situations of over-fueling that cause engine power loss are eliminated.
- **Less pollution**: as no excess is generated, the mixture burns completely, without generating as much waste.
- **Increased air intake**: by eliminating the carburetor, which offers resistance to the passage of air (this is the basis of the Venturi principle), the air enters the cylinder freely.
- **Improved cold starting**: the control unit is capable of dosing the necessary amount of gasoline for cold starting.

Parts of the injection system

The injection system is composed of several elements, all of which are indispensable for its correct operation:

- **Injector**: this is a solenoid valve that sprays gasoline at the precise moment and quantity required by the cylinder. They are located in the intake nozzle, just before the valve of the same name.

Picture 71.   Injector

- **Air flow meter or flow meter**: indicates to the control unit the amount of air entering the engine.
- **Control unit**: receives the information from the sensors and sends the opening order to the injectors. It tells them when and how long they have to open.
- **Gasoline pump**: transports gasoline from the tank to the injectors. It is electric. To avoid blockages in the injectors, it has a filter.

- 🦎 **Pressure regulator**: this is a solenoid valve located between the pump and the injector to ensure that the injector pressure is adequate.
- 🦎 **Contact box**: informs the control unit of the position of the throttle valve, which is the one we can control from the throttle.
- 🦎 **Crankshaft sensor**: necessary to determine where the piston is inside the cylinder, and whether we are accelerating or decelerating.
- 🦎 **Coolant temperature sensor**: adapts the mixture to the engine operating temperature.

9.4 The air filter

Although it may seem a minor element, and many are determined to remove them, the air filter performs a vital task: it protects our engine from the entry of impurities.

Although we do not see them, there are numerous particles in the air we breathe. Even more so if we drive on dusty roads.

We have already explained the importance of lubrication to avoid wear of parts that are in continuous friction. Imagine now that we introduce a sandpaper between the piston and the cylinder liner. This is what happens when a particle of sand penetrates the cylinder: it will end up scratching it.

We have also explained how a carburetor, or an injector works, and how extremely fine their ducts are. Any impurity that penetrates with the intake air could clog them.

For this reason, an air filter is always placed at the engine air inlet (before the carburetor and injectors).

They are made of paper or fiber (foam filters), which allow air to pass through, but are capable of retaining very fine particles.

It is not worth stretching the life of an air filter beyond the miles recommended by the manufacturer, since its price is not expensive, and its function is vital.

Picture 72.   Air filters

A dirty or clogged air filter will cause the amount of air reaching the cylinder to be much less than recommended.

The conical air filters, so fashionable nowadays thanks to the Cafe Racer trend, pick up the gauntlet of the designs of the past, to adapt them to modern motorcycles, however, almost in the totality of the occasions they diminish the performances of the engine and increase its noises.

✂ Air filter change

As we have seen, keeping an air filter in good condition and clean is essential to ensure good motorcycle performance.

For this reason, it is recommended to change it <u>every 6,000 mi / 10.000 km</u>.

The procedure will depend on the motorcycle, as in each model it may be housed in one compartment or another, but always look for it behind the engine and carburetor.

Its replacement will be limited to accessing it, loosening it from its anchorages and installing the new filter.

It is usually not worthwhile to clean or blow it out, as these are inexpensive items on which it does not pay to skimp.

Filters made of paper cannot be reused once they have reached their useful life. Those made of synthetic fiber can be washed and reused.

9.5   Gasoline tank

I'm not going to dwell too much on the gas tank. We all know what it is for and how it works.

This is a tank usually made of steel or fiberglass that contains the gasoline that feeds the engine.

It has a lid on its upper part that allows quick access to fill it with fuel.

In its lower part there are one or more stopcocks that allow the gasoline to reach the carburetor or injectors by gravity. It is at this point that the fuel filter is housed, which prevents impurities in the fuel, or those that have come out of the tank, from ending up in the carburetor or injectors.

In addition, inside it contains a gauge that sends a signal to the motorcycle's control unit with the level of gasoline remaining.

9.6   Power system failures

Fuel system failures are very common, especially on carburetor-powered motorcycles.

This is due to the fact that they are elements that must be adjusted frequently, so that any maladjustment is immediately noticeable in the performance of the motorcycle.

1) Poor carburation

Incorrect adjustment of one, several or all of the carburetors significantly affects the performance of the motorcycle.

Among its consequences are the following:

- Unable to start the motorcycle.
- Lack of response when accelerating.
- Idle out of rhythm.
- Black spark plugs.
- Excess gasoline consumption.
- Increased contamination.
- Black smoke in the exhaust.
- Engine overheating.

To make it clear, the carburetor regulates the engine's power supply. If we assimilate it to the human body, a failure in our power supply can affect all the systems of our body.

A fine adjustment of a carburetor must be made in a workshop using vacuum gauges, elements capable of measuring the pressure in the carburetor ducts.

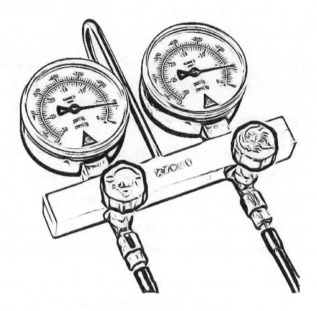

Picture 73.   Vacuum gauge

As beginner mechanics we can regulate the carburetion by means of the screws that, for this purpose, exist in our carburetor, and that we have explained in the chapter "Regulation of the carburetion".

Remember that this must always be done when the motorcycle is warm, although if you cannot start it, you will have no choice but to do it when it is cold.

2) Flooded motorcycle

It used to be very common to hear "you're going to flood the bike" when you tried to start the bike unsuccessfully for a long time.

This expression means to bring an excess of gasoline into the cylinder, usually by trying to start a motorcycle cold for a long time, introducing a lot of gasoline, but little air into the engine.

It can also be caused by a fault in the carburetor or injector, which provides a mixture that is too rich.

The solution, unless you have a poorly adjusted carburetor, is very simple: wait for the gasoline to evaporate.

3) **Faulty injector**

The advantage of injectors over carburetors is that they require almost no maintenance, being able to electronically maintain the correct mixture dosage.

However, the injectors are vulnerable to surges. Be sure to disconnect the battery for charging and always keep the battery terminals tight.

Although I do not recommend that you touch the injectors if you do not have some knowledge of mechanics, they also have several mixture regulation screws, which you can tighten or loosen for proper dosing.

An injector failure is usually associated with an electronic malfunction, either in the injector connection or in the electronic injection control unit.

4) **Throttle cable breakage**

This is a relatively common failure, especially on older motorcycles.

The throttle cable connects the throttle grip to the carburetor bell, being subjected to constant stretching and winding, which eventually deteriorates and breaks it.

The consequence is disastrous, as it paralyzes the motorcycle, however, the repair is not costly or complicated, as it is simply a matter of replacing the cable with the same one and it is not usually difficult to install.

It is important to place the cable exactly along its path, otherwise it is easy to inadvertently accelerate the bike when turning the handlebars.

5) Carburetor diaphragm rupture

Diaphragm carburetors let more or less air through depending on the cylinder suction.

They do this thanks to membranes located in the upper part of the carburetor, which work by vacuum effect. It is very common that, over time, they end up cracking.

You will notice a loss of performance of the bike, especially when accelerating, as the bike will not respond immediately.

The solution is very simple: open the carburetor hood and replace the membrane, which must be perfectly positioned.

Picture 74.   Carburetor diaphragm

6) Cracked rubbers

It may seem silly, but a large number of carburetion problems disappear when all the rubber parts of the system are in good condition.

Plastic materials, subjected to inclement weather and the action of the sun, eventually dry out and crack, especially if exposed to the corrosive action of gasoline.

This causes small cracks to appear where gasoline drips (easily detectable) or where small amounts of air enter (very difficult to detect).

The solution is immediate and inexpensive: change tubes and rubbers when you see them cracked, stiff and dry.

10 Exhaust Pipe

The exhaust pipe is the element in charge of evacuating the gases produced during the explosion of the mixture inside the combustion chamber.

We can summarize the functions of the exhaust pipe as follows:

- 🏍 To evacuate the combustion gases produced inside the cylinder and facilitate their exit.
- 🏍 Decrease the temperature of these gases, since they leave the cylinder at more than 300 degrees.
- 🏍 Reduce the sound of explosions.
- 🏍 Reduce the amount of polluting particles emitted into the atmosphere.

*In the old days, each cylinder had its own exhaust pipe, which made for impressive bikes, such as the **Benelli Sei.***

Picture 75.   Benelli 750 Sei

Nowadays, it is common for motorcycles with more than one cylinder to group the exhaust gas outlets in common manifolds. Thus, it is common to find configurations of 2 in 1, 4 in 1, 4 in 2 or 6 in 2.

10.1 Evacuation of gases

The geometry of the exhaust pipe is of vital importance, since it is not only a matter of achieving a fast (and as soundless as possible) exhaust gas exit, but the exhaust pipe helps to orient and pace the pressure waves that occur when the exhaust valve opens, so that they, in turn, favor the extraction of gases from the following explosions.

In other words, the wave produced in the first explosion helps to extract the gases from the following explosions. For this reason, it is counterproductive to ride "free exhaust".

This is especially relevant at high rpm, since the time the exhaust valve remains open is minimal. At this time, a little help to "pull" the gases out of the cylinder is vital.

To understand this, without going into the theoretical component of the study of pressure waves, we can imagine a human chain to extinguish a fire, taking buckets of water from a pool. From the first person starts a bucket full of water. When it reaches the last person, he throws the water away, but the bucket returns (the smoke goes out, but a wave returns), when that bucket reaches the first person again, that bucket (which is the first one that went out) helps to take more water out of the pool (that wave that has returned helps to take smoke out of the cylinder).

Motorcycle brands take advantage of this circumstance for the design of their exhaust pipes, and modern motorcycles include valves that decrease the exhaust section at low revolutions, thus increasing the exit velocity. When the revolutions increase, the valve opens the entire available section.

The geometry of the exhaust pipe and its length is essential to achieve the desired effect, both in terms of exhaust wave utilization and reduction of noise and pollutants.

10.2 Noise reduction

Another primary function of the exhaust pipe is to reduce the noise caused by the exhaust gases and the sound waves produced by the explosion (which also escape from the cylinder through the exhaust valve).

The part of the exhaust that is responsible for reducing the noise level is called the **muffler or silencer** and is the final part of the exhaust pipe.

There are different types of mufflers depending on their geometry, but in essence, their function is to interpose physical barriers to the sound waves, so that when they reach the end of the exhaust, they are attenuated. These barriers cannot, as far as possible, hinder the exit of gases.

Picture 76.   Silencer Supertrapp IDS2 for Suzuki

In the past, it was necessary to renew the silencer, since its fiber components had a limited life. Nowadays, they are manufactured in materials that, although they require proper maintenance, do not require replacement.

10.3 Reduction of pollutants

Another function of the exhaust pipe is to reduce the amount of polluting particles that we expel into the atmosphere. Think that the exhaust pipe works as a chimney that expels the smoke of combustion, so it contains a large amount of pollutants. To reduce them, an element called **catalytic** converter or catalytic converter is installed.

This is a mesh of a ceramic product (composed of platinum, rhodium and palladium) which, when in contact with combustion fumes, causes chemical reactions that transform harmful compounds into carbon dioxide, water vapor, molecular nitrogen and oxygen. It is located upstream of the muffler.

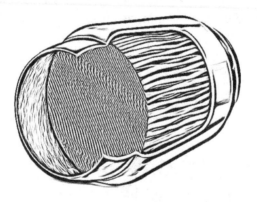

Picture 77.   Exhaust catalytic converter

10.4 What does the color of our motorcycle's smoke indicate?

The color (and smell) of the smoke coming out of our exhaust can be a great indicator of the health of our engine. Below, we will review the symptoms that can cause exhaust smoke to take on a certain color.

🏍 **Black smoke:** the mixture is too <u>rich in gasoline </u>(fat mixture), i.e., the carburetor or the injectors are letting more gasoline through than necessary, which does not burn completely. It will be enough to regulate the carburetor or the injectors (or to repair them) or to make a good adjustment of valves. An excess of gasoline in the mixture can also be caused by air defect, which is to say, an adequate amount of gasoline enters, but there is not enough air to burn it. This may be due to a dirty or clogged air filter. This smoke smells like gasoline and "stings" in the throat.

If it only appears when a strong acceleration is given, we should not worry, it may be due to accumulated carbon or an instantaneous excess of gasoline.

🏍 **White smoke:** usually means that there is <u>water in the exhaust</u>. It is common that the smoke comes out white as soon as you start your motorcycle, especially if it has slept outdoors or if the temperature is low. It is due to the condensation of water on the cooler surface of the exhaust. Condensation smoke does not smell of anything.

If the smoke comes out white continuously and does not go away, it may be due to the presence of <u>water in the engine</u>, due to a failure in the cooling system. The liquid can enter through a deteriorated cylinder head gasket, and this is a serious problem. In this case, the smoke is not oily (put your hand on the exhaust outlet, without touching it of course!) and has a sweet smell.

🏍 **Blue smoke:** bluish smoke denotes the presence of <u>oil in the engine</u>. It may be due to the poor condition of the piston rings (they do not seal the combustion chamber and the oil from the

143

crankcase rises inside the cylinder) or to a broken valve O-ring. In addition to the color, the smoke will smell of burnt oil.

If the smoke appears when accelerating, it is likely to be a valve problem. If, on the other hand, it appears when reducing, it may be a piston ring problem.

Be careful if your motorcycle is a two-stroke. It will always burn oil, since it will be mixed in the gasoline. If it is not a radical change in the amount of smoke, there is no need to worry.

11 The Wheels

The wheels are the basis of the movement of our motorcycle, without them there would be no movement. There is no need to recall how important their discovery was for humanity.

In the case of motorcycles, and this is precisely what characterizes them, we have two wheels, a rear drive wheel and a front steering wheel. Unlike cars, motorcycles are always rear-wheel drive (with the exception of some minority inventions such as the VeloSoleX).

The wheel consists of the rim (rim in some Latin American countries) and the tire. Inside the tire there may be an inner tube, or the tire itself may hold pressurized air inside (tubeless system).

The original rims (and still some current ones of classic design) were made of spokes. Thin metal cylinders that joined the rim to the pivot axle or hub. With the passage of time, and especially with the increase in motorcycle performance, the spokes have been replaced by metal elements of greater strength and rigidity.

11.1 Tire parts

The tire keeps us glued to the road, whether in dry conditions or in waterlogged mud. That's why its composition and design is no easy task.

Tires are composed of a tread (the part that sticks to the road), a bead (the part that sticks to the rim) and a sidewall or shoulder, which is the profile of the tire.

The tread is responsible for evacuating the water from the road that the tire treads on, for which it has channels forming a "pattern". In tires intended for road or off-road driving, the tread has very deep and pronounced grooves, forming lugs.

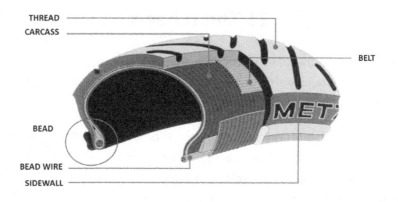

Picture 78.   Tire parts

11.2 What the tire codes mean

Whenever we see a tire, whether it is a motorcycle or a car tire, we will distinguish a succession of numbers and letters with no apparent meaning. These codes provide us with valuable information that we will see below.

On the (car) tire shown by Michelin, we find the code **205/45 R16 83 V.**

Picture 79.   Tire code

- The first number (**205**) refers to the width of our tire, measured in millimeters.
- The second (**45**) refers to the ratio between the tire profile (from the rim to the ground) and the tire width, in percent. In

this example, the profile is 45% of the width (0.45*205=92.25 mm).

- 🏍 **R** indicates the diameter of the rim on which the tire will be mounted, measured in inches, **16** in this case.
- 🏍 **83** indicates the maximum load of the vehicle. It is a two-digit code ranging from 20 to 87, which you can determine in the table below.
- 🏍 **V indicates a** high-speed tire (see other codes in the table below).

Load index

Index	kg	Index	kg	Index	kg
42	150	68	315	89	580
44	160	69	325	90	600
46	170	70	335	91	615
47	175	71	345	92	630
48	180	72	355	93	650
50	190	73	365	94	670
51	195	74	375	95	690
52	200	75	387	96	710
53	206	76	400	97	730
54	212	77	412	98	750
55	218	78	425	99	775
58	236	79	437	100	800
59	243	80	450	101	825
60	250	81	462	102	850
61	257	82	475	103	875
62	265	83	487	104	900
63	272	84	500	105	925
64	280	85	515	106	950
65	290	86	530	107	975
66	300	87	545	108	1000
67	307	88	560		

Speed index

Index	Km h	Index	Km h	Index	Km h	Index	Km h
A1	5	B	50	L	120	U	200
A2	10	C	60	M	130	H	210
A3	15	D	65	N	140	V	240
A4	20	E	70	P	150	ZR	>240
A5	25	F	80	Q	160	W	270
A6	30	G	90	R	170	Y	300
A7	35	J	100	S	180		
A8	40	K	110	T	190		

How to read tires in inches?

You may be wondering: the code of my tires, or of the tires I have seen on the web does not look anything like the 205/45 R16 type.

In that case your tire is in inches. For example: *Firestone Deluxe 5.00-16 71P.*

It is telling you that the width of the tire is 5 inches (1 inch is 25.4 mm so the width of your tire is 127 mm, which is equivalent to a 130).

Classic tires were round to allow the use of tubes, i.e., their width is equal to their profile. In other words, their profile is 100% of their width. With this we already have the second digit: 100.

The last one is quite easy, because it already comes in inches: 16 inches.

Forgetting 71P, which refers to tire load and speed, we have a 130/100 R16. Easy, isn't it?

In any case, I leave you a table of equivalences to make it easier for you to check.

Inches			Millimeters	
Diameter	Normal Series	Reduced Series	90 series	90 series
16"	3,25-16		100/90-16	110/80-16
	3,50-10	4,60-16	110/90-16	120/80-16
			120/90-16	
	5,00-16	5,10-16	130/90-16	150/80-16
17"	2,5-17	3,10-17	80/90-17	
	2,75-17	3,10-17	80/90-17	
	4,25-17		120/90-17	130/80-17
	4,50-17	5,10-17	130/90-17	140/80-17
18"	2,50-18			
	2,75-18	3,10-18	80/90-18	
	3,00-18	3,10-18	80/90-18	
	3,25-18	3,60-18	90/90-18	100/80-18
	3,50-18	4,10-18	100/90-18	110/80-18
	3,75-18	4,10-18	100/90-18	110/80-18
	4,00-18	4,25/85-18	110/90-18	120/80-18
	4,25-18		130/90-18	130/80-18
		4,60-18	120/90-18	140/80-18
19"	3,00-19			
	3,25-19		90/90-19	
	3,50-19	4,10-19	100/90-19	
			110/90-19	
21"	2,75-21		80/90-21	
	3,00-21		90/90-21	

11.3 Types of tires

In addition to the already mentioned knobby tires or road tires, we can classify tires by their structure: we distinguish **diagonal and radial** tires.

Bias-ply tires have their compounds arranged diagonally to the direction of travel, with one ply overlapping the other. This was the usual form of tire construction until a few years ago. When they "stepped" on each other, the tires heated up unevenly, especially at high speeds, which led to deformation.

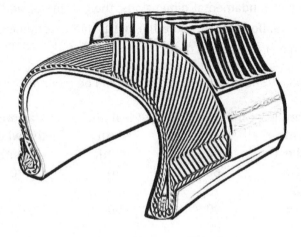

Picture 80.   Bias-ply tire

To avoid this, <u>radial tires</u> were created, with compounds perpendicular to the direction of travel (spoke or radial direction), which have ostensibly improved the qualities of the tires.

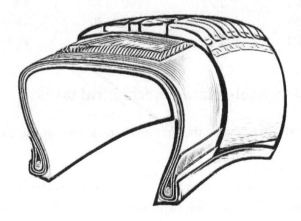

Picture 81.   Radial tire

11.4 Tires compatible with each rim

Tires have two fundamental dimensions, their diameter and the width of their groove. Both are measured in inches and determine the type of tire that can be mounted on them.

The table below shows the tire width that can be mounted on each rim.

Rim width (inches)	Minimum tire width (mm)	Ideal tire width (mm)	Maximum tire width (mm)
1,60	60	70	80
1,85	70	80	90
2,15	80	90	110
2,50	90	110 - 120	130
2,75	100	110 - 120	140
3,00	110	120 - 130	140
3,50	120	130 - 140	150
4,00	130	140 - 150	160
4,50	150	150 - 160	170
5,00	150	160 - 170	190
5,50	160	170 - 180	190
6,00	170	180 - 190	200

11.5 Basic wheel-related mechanical tasks

Fixing a flat tire is probably the first mechanical task we all learn, even if we do it on a bicycle.

That's when the passion for mechanics awakens within us, which can lead us to be reading this book right now.

Wheels never stop rolling, withstand bumps, our weight and the way we drive, so they are exposed to a large number of failures.

Here are the ones you will be able to solve without going to a mechanic.

1) Disassemble a wheel 🔧

Removing a wheel is one of the simplest mechanical tasks.

Although some manufacturers try to make it difficult, it usually boils down to loosening a couple of screws.

If it is the front wheel you will have to pay special attention to the brake calipers, which should separate from the disc easily without the need to remove any bolts.

The rear wheel is always more difficult to remove because it is usually more difficult to access.

Locate the chain tensioner and loosen it. Remove the bolts and axle and the wheel should come off without a problem, although you may have to lift the bike to save the fenders.

Normally it will not be necessary to remove the chain, belt or cardan shaft, as they are usually mounted on an independent group, precisely to allow the wheel to be removed.

If you have a drum brake, you will have to unscrew the rod that actuates it.

When reassembling the wheels, always remember to apply the brake several times to return the brake pads to their position.

2) Change a tire 🔧

If you have removed the wheel, it is usually to fix a puncture or to change a tire for a new one.

Personally, I usually take my bike to the shop for any tire change or puncture repair.

Because of the cost it has, it is not usually worth doing it myself, since every day it is more complicated to extract the tires if you do not have special machines.

Once you have dismounted the wheel you have to bead it. This means to separate the tire bead from the rim.

For this purpose, garages use bead breaking machines and you, I am afraid, will have to make do with a manual bead breaker.

Picture 82.   Shop floor bead breaker

Picture 83.   Manual bead breaker

It is true that you can do it using flat screwdrivers or the classic removable ones usually used on bicycles, but you have to be very careful not to deform the beads, especially in tubeless tires, as they will lose their watertightness.

Picture 84.   Set of dismountable

For tire mounting and demounting, it is advisable to use a specific paste for this purpose (sometimes, with very hard tires, it is indispensable). Its function is to soften the tire and lubricate it, facilitating the tasks of bead breaking, dismounting and later mounting.

By the way, when you mount the tire again, locate the arrow indicating the direction of rotation, don't mount it backwards.

3) Fix a puncture ⚒

This is something we learn as children when we are given our first bike.

At least in the past, now we tend to take our bikes to the workshop more and more often.

However, fixing a puncture is a simple task on a bike, which can turn into a real hell on a motorcycle.

If your wheels are tubeless, i.e., without an inner tube, the task is simpler, as you do not have to dismount the tire.

Just buy a **tire repair kit**, they are inexpensive and easy to use:

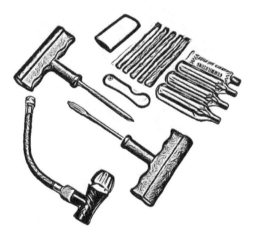

Picture 85.   Puncture repair kit

1) Without removing the wheel, locate the puncture. Usually, you will be able to see a stone, or a nail embedded in the tire.
2) Remove the nail or stone, if possible, with pliers, so that nothing is left inside.
3) If you do not locate the puncture, you will have to disassemble the wheel and put it in a water bath until you see the bubbles.
4) Insert the punch from the kit fearlessly into the puncture and rotate it to enlarge the hole and sand the edges.
5) Insert the rubber band into the needle-like tool.
6) Insert the tool with the rubber band into the puncture, so that both ends of the rubber band are facing outward.
7) Pull out the tool.
8) Use a box cutter or scissors to cut off any protruding part of the tire. Do not leave it too flush.
9) Fill the tire with air to check for air leaks.
10) Roll carefully so that the rubber band vulcanizes and adheres properly to your wheel.

To repair a puncture on a tubed wheel, you must disassemble the wheel and tire:

1) Dismount the wheel.
2) Deflate the wheel.
3) Dismount the tire.
4) Inflate the tire to locate the puncture (the easiest way to do this is to soak the tube in a water bath).
5) Sand the surface of the puncture.
6) Apply glue.
7) Place the patch.
8) Apply pressure.
9) Reassemble everything.

4) Balancing a wheel ✗

The normal use of a motorcycle causes the tires to wear unevenly.

Also, a small (or not so small) bump can produce small irregularities in the tires that can cause them to be out of balance.

To balance a wheel (although it is something they do at the shop every time we change tires) you must:

1) Remove the wheel from the motorcycle.
2) Place it in a location where the wheel can rotate freely.
3) Make sure that one point is below the rest, i.e., that the wheel has a certain drop to one point. This will be quite easy if the wheel can be completely vertical.
4) Turn the wheel and let it stop by itself.
5) Make a mark on the part of the tire that has stopped at the low point.
6) Repeat the operation: if the wheel always stops in the same place, it is badly balanced. If it stops in a different place each time, it is well balanced.
7) Place a counterweight just opposite the mark on the rim.
8) Repeat the operation until the wheel is fully balanced.

Picture 86.   Balancing counterweights

12 Brakes

I don't need to explain to you what the brakes are for. If they fail you, you'll be in a lot of trouble that only good reflexes will get you out of.

In this chapter we will analyze the different braking systems that can be fitted to a motorcycle and their most common failures.

Leaving aside old systems such as rod brakes, skid brakes or cantilever brakes, there are three major braking systems:

a) Caliper brakes

b) Drum brakes

c) Disc brakes

In addition to these three systems that we will analyze in depth, it is important to know that there are two ways to transmit braking force from your hand to the wheel or from your foot to the wheel:

a) Mechanical brakes: the force is transmitted by cables or levers. When you squeeze the brake lever, you pull a cable that activates the brake.

b) Hydraulic brakes: most of today's brakes are usually hydraulic. The force is transmitted through a fluid, called brake fluid. When the brake lever is squeezed, the fluid is pushed, which will end up pushing the brake and stopping the wheel of the motorcycle. Its operation is similar to that of a syringe.

12.1 Types of brakes

a) Classic caliper brakes

Although, as we will see a little later, drum brakes also have brake shoes, by this type of brake I mean the traditional bicycle brakes, with a clamp that grips the wheel on both sides when we press the brake lever. They can also be called horseshoe brakes, because of the shape of the caliper, or shoe brakes.

They are the most basic brakes, and also the ones that brake the least.

Its operation is quite simple. By squeezing the lever, we tighten a cable that closes the clamp around the wheel, slowing it down. It is as if we had giant pliers, and we close it on the wheel.

They are not currently installed on any motorcycle, but you may find them on a very classic motorcycle.

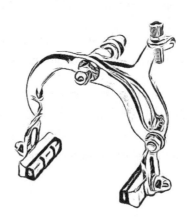

Picture 87.   Caliper brake

b) Drum brakes

They are common on older motorcycles and small-displacement motorcycles, especially on their rear wheels.

They are called internal expansion brakes, now we will see why.

To brake, they use curved steel parts covered by a rough material, called lining. The assembly is called a brake shoe.

In this case, the system expands inside a metal cylinder in the center of the wheel, called a drum. As it expands, the brake shoes rub against the inside of the drum, eventually braking the wheel.

Imagine that you are a child again and you play hula hoop (for the record, I have never played, but it is a good example). The hoop is spinning around your waist, at increasing speed (it's the wheel). At a given moment, we want to stop the hoop, and we open our arms. The arms, as they open, come in contact with the hoop, stopping it. The arms would be the brake shoes.

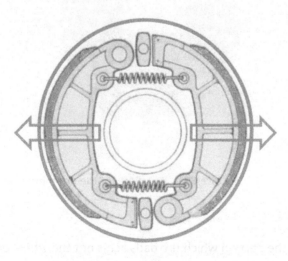

Picture 88.   Drum brake operation

161

They are usually used as rear brakes, as they require less braking power than front brakes and do not heat up as much.

It is important to know that temperature influences friction, so at elevated temperatures, our drum brake will stop braking properly. This is the main disadvantage of this brake system, since it is difficult to cool as it is inside the wheel. In addition, the need to ventilate the brake is detrimental to the need to keep them dry. These brakes also perform poorly in the wet.

The part that holds and keeps the brake shoes fixed is called the brake shoe carrier plate. The drum, unlike the caliper brakes, rotates jointly with the wheel.

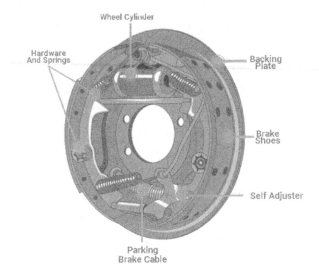

Picture 89.   Parts of the drum brake

c) Disc brakes

In this case, the part on which the pads act is not the wheel or the inside of a drum, but a steel disc.

If you have noticed, we are no longer talking about brake shoes but about brake pads. Brake pads are flat pieces of steel coated with a porous material that grips the steel very well.

When we exert pressure on the braking circuit, we are pushing a pair of brake pads against a disc, which will try to stop it by all means, pressing one on each side.

Imagine a basketball flying towards your body. The ball will be our disc. You will open your hands and, at the right moment, you will close them against the ball, slamming on the brakes and preventing it from hitting your body (your face in the worst case). Your hands are the brake pads.

All the force used to brake the bike by rubbing the pads against the disc is released in the form of heat (the disc gets hot), that's why they have so many holes, to help dissipate that heat.

Picture 90.   Brake disc

The pads are arranged in pairs, clamping the disc, inside metal elements that hold them in position and are called brake calipers. The pads are pushed by cylindrical steel parts, called pistons, which are also placed in pairs (on both sides of the disc). Thus, we can find calipers with 2, 4 or 6 pistons.

The disc brake is, today, the best braking system. By squeezing the disc from both sides (unlike the drum, which only squeezes from the inside), a greater braking force is applied.

Another advantage of the disc brake is that it is external to the wheel, which allows it to dissipate heat and moisture.

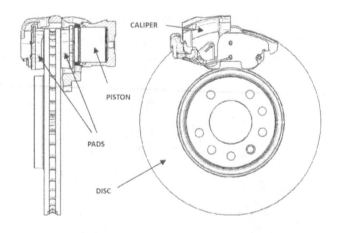

Picture 91.   Disc brake

12.2 How does a hydraulic brake work?

It is important to know how a hydraulic brake works, especially to understand possible malfunctions.

As noted above, its basis is similar to that of a syringe. When we squeeze at one end, we transmit pressure to the other end. This pressure is transmitted particle to particle and is explained by Pascal's Principle.

Although its understanding is beyond the scope of a basic mechanics manual like this one, I'll leave its statement in case you want to score a goal the next time you see your brother-in-law:

> *"The pressure exerted on an incompressible fluid at equilibrium inside a vessel with non-deformable walls is transmitted with equal intensity in all directions and at all points of the fluid"*

As the brake circuit has non-deformable walls and the brake fluid is incompressible (all taken to the ideal world, of course), when we press the brake lever or step on the brake pedal we are applying a force that is transmitted through the brake hoses until it reaches the caliper. In the caliper there are cylinders (pistons) that push the pads against the disc, braking the wheel. The component that transmits our force to the fluid is called the brake pump.

The problems come when we include in the circuit elements that can be compressed, such as an air bubble, but we will see this in the next chapter.

12.3 The ABS system

High-performance motorcycles are usually fitted with an ABS braking system. The acronym ABS stands for *Anti-lock Braking System*.

When we encounter an obstacle and want to slam on the brakes, we press hard on the brakes (and close our eyes).

In this situation, the wheels usually lock up and a skid or skidding occurs. At that moment we lose control of our motorcycle, and no matter how hard we press on the brakes we will not be able to stop, in addition to losing control over the steering.

This is prevented by a system that avoids wheel locking.

So to speak, even if we keep the lever fully depressed, the ABS system brakes in a staggered manner, in pulses, thus preventing the wheel from locking and the motorcycle from skidding.

This can be seen very well in ABS skid marks because it leaves a dashed line on the asphalt.

Picture 92.   Skid marks with ABS

ABS systems have a control unit capable of measuring very precisely the rotational speed of the motorcycle's wheels. When it detects a deceleration of the wheel (when braking) above the skidding limits, it sends an order to the brake to stop working until the deceleration limits are recovered. This happens in a matter of milliseconds, so it achieves a lot of braking per second. This prevents the wheel from locking up under hard braking.

12.4 Typical brake malfunctions

The brakes require important maintenance, as they are responsible for stopping our motorcycle in the event of an obstacle appearing in our path.

1) Worn pads or shoes

The degree of wear of the brake pads or shoes should be checked periodically. A worn pad or shoe has two harmful effects on our motorcycle:

1. They stop braking.
2. They spoil the discs and drums.

The first effect is obvious. If the rough layer that manages to stop the wheel thanks to its high coefficient of friction disappears, we will be rubbing two metal parts against each other, which will slide without braking.

The second effect is the result of what I have just told you. Under the layer of porous material appears the piece of steel that forms the pad that, instead of stopping the disc or the drum, will scratch it and damage it.

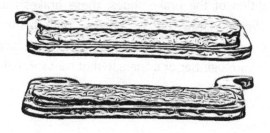

Picture 93.   New vs. worn pads

Checking the degree of wear is a simple task. For disc brakes, just look at the caliper from the front. On both sides of the disc you will see some brown or dark gray parts, these are the brake pads.

You will see that they have two colors, the part in contact with the disc is the material that brakes and the part farther away from the disc is the material that supports the pad.

The tablet should never be **less than 1 mm** thick. When you see that they start to be too thin, change them. In any case, you will have noticed it beforehand, as you will hear an unpleasant squeaking noise when braking.

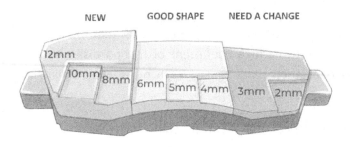

Picture 94.   Levels for changing brake pads

In the case of drum brakes, to avoid having to remove the wheel to check the condition of the brake shoes, these brakes usually have a warning light. We will know that we have to replace the pads when, while the brake is at rest, the brake cam points to the indicator (usually two arrows that join together or a triangle that runs through a delimited area).

Picture 95.   Limit of use of drum brake

Brake shoes last much longer than brake pads, mainly because you brake much less with the rear brake than with the front brake.

2) Change brake pads 🔧

Changing a motorcycle's brake pads is a fairly simple task.

On average, it is usually done **every 9,000 mi / 15.000 km**, however, it absolutely depends on our driving style.

1. First you must make sure you buy exactly the right pads for your bike (you can find them with your VIN or with the exact model of your bike on the internet).
2. Disassemble the calipers by removing the bolts that attach them to the suspension. It is not necessary to remove the hose attached to the caliper, in fact, do not remove it, or you will fill everything with brake fluid.

Picture 96.   Disassemble calipers

3.   Remove the top cover to expose the pad retaining system. Sometimes it will be a simple spring with a rod and sometimes you will have to remove another screw.

4.   Pull the pads out of the caliper, using a flat screwdriver. They should come out almost by themselves by hand, from the bottom of the caliper.

5.   Thoroughly clean the inside of the caliper, if possible with an air compressor and brake cleaner.

6.   Force the pistons with your hand until you push them a little into their cavity. The new pads are thicker than the worn ones, so the piston cannot stay in the same position it was in.

7.   Place the new pads in the same position as the ones you just removed. Be careful not to stain the new pads with grease or brake fluid as the pads are very absorbent and would lose braking efficiency.

8.   Replace the clamping screw, the cover and screw the calipers back to the suspension. Do not overtighten the clamp bolts. If you overtighten the clamp bolts, you will lose a bolt that should last a lifetime.

When changing the pads, try to ride carefully at first, until they adapt properly.

A used disc does not have an exact geometry, but usually has certain imperfections or bends, and the pads have to adapt until they brake normally.

It is important to bear in mind that the pads must be changed all at the same time, not only the most worn ones. If some are changed and others are not, the geometry of the system will be unbalanced, affecting braking and damaging the new pads and the disc.

3) Change brake shoe ✂

Changing the brake shoe is much more complicated than changing the brake pad, at least much more cumbersome, since you have to disassemble the entire wheel.

Once the brake is removed from the drum, you have to loosen the springs that keep them shrunk, unscrew the old brake shoes and install the new ones.

If you have squeezed the old brake shoes to the limit, the tensioner will be at full tension and the bike will be slowed down when the drum is replaced.

4) Braking noise

If you hear an unpleasant squeaking noise when braking, it is most likely that you have worn out your brake pads or brake shoes, so you should replace them with new ones.

It is also common that some dirt has been trapped in the intermediate part of the brake pad. Remove the calipers and remove any stones or impurities using a screwdriver. On a drum brake you will have to remove the wheel completely to clean it.

A bent or scratched disc can also cause an unpleasant noise when braking.

Finally, even if the brake pads look still unworn, if they are many years old (and few miles) it is possible that they have crystallized. In that case, they will have lost all braking efficiency and will probably squeak when braking.

5) Vibration during braking

If, in addition to noises, you notice vibrations when braking, the cause may be irregular wear of the brake pads or brake shoes or, in a worse case, of the disc.

In this case, the solution is to replace the deformed parts.

6) Worn discs

If you have been over-tightening without changing the pads, it is possible that your disc has been scratched.

When wear is so severe that its resistance is in danger, it should be replaced by a new one.

This occurs on average **every 35,000 mi / 60.000 km**, although it will depend on your driving style and the maintenance of the other braking components.

Picture 97.   Shredded disc

Discs are considerably more expensive than pads but, fortunately, they wear much more slowly.

7) Bent discs

A bad hit in an accident, a fall or simply tying the bike to a hard element can bend the brake disc.

In this case, it will be the disc that will damage the pads, calipers and the whole system, preventing braking.

It is necessary to replace it with a new one.

8) Improperly vented hydraulic circuit

One of the most common failures of any hydraulic brake is the presence of bubbles in the circuit.

You will notice it because the lever has a spongy feel when braking or because, in spite of pressing it hard, the bike does not brake as it should.

As explained above, the transmission of forces in a fluid is based on the fluid being incompressible, i.e., it does not change volume when a force is applied to it. This applies to brake fluid, which is specifically designed so that, when it receives pressure from the brake pump, it transmits it multiplied to the pistons in the brake calipers.

An air bubble does not work in the same way. When we introduce a bubble into a brake circuit, it acts as a cushion.

Air, unlike brake fluid, is compressible. When a force is applied to the air bubble, it reduces its volume, it is crushed.

All that volume that is compressed by the air in the circuit is the distance that the pads are leaving to travel on the disc. In short, if there is air in the circuit, your bike will not brake.

🔧 Brake bleeding

The action of removing the air from the brake circuit is called bleeding and, fortunately, it is very simple. Here are the steps:

1. Locate the bleeder on the brake caliper. It is a small bolt at the top, with a drilled head.

Picture 98.   Brake circuit bleeder

2. Get a flexible and transparent tube, the size of the bleeder head and place it over it. Place a canister at the end of the tube, to avoid staining with brake fluid (it is really corrosive and toxic).

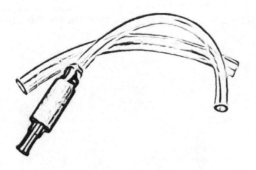

Picture 99.   Flexible rubber tubing

3. Open the brake pump cap (you will find the front one on the handlebars next to the brake lever and the rear one behind the brake pedal).

4. Make sure you have plenty of brake fluid in the pump (usually it will be DOT4 type). If it is below its minimum level, top up with brake fluid.

5. Tighten the brake lever. Leave it tight, either by hand or with a rubber band.

6. Slowly loosen the bleeder with a flat wrench until you see liquid and bubbles coming out of the bleeder tube.

7. Close the bleeder.

8. Release the lever and refill the reservoir, which will be lowered. Never allow air to enter through the reservoir or, in other words, never run out of fluid in the reservoir.

9. Repeat the process until you check that no bubbles come out when you open the bleeder.

A complete brake fluid change is recommended **every 2 years or every 15,000 mi / 25.000 km**, although it is usually done when its coloration has become very dark.

By the way, there are vacuum pumps that make the purging task much easier.

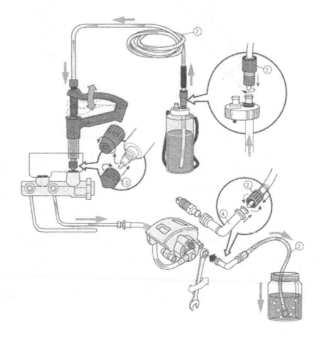

Picture 100.   Vacuum pump purging

9) Hoses in bad condition

The second condition of Pascal's principle for forces to be transmitted in a liquid was that the walls should be non-deformable.

This is simple to understand. If we place a balloon filled with water on a deformable surface, for example, plasticine, and exert pressure on the balloon, the plasticine will not deform, since the balloon will absorb the deformation.

If the same amount of water is introduced into a non-deformable element, such as a glass bottle, all the pressure will be exerted on the plasticine, deforming it.

The same applies to the hoses. The hoses are usually made of Teflon, a polymer that, although it withstands a lot of weathering, eventually weakens and cracks.

When it loses its properties, it ends up becoming deformable, so it can absorb part of the force that we transmit through the brake pump.

The solution is to replace the hoses with new ones. Metal hoses have fewer disadvantages.

It is advisable to change the hoses of your bike at least **every 4 years**. To be honest, I change them when I notice that the bike doesn't brake as well as it did at the beginning and I've discarded everything else, which is usually after many more years or never.

10) Tensioning of brakes

It is important to know that all brake systems can be tensioned.

When you notice that your bike does not brake as well as it used to, before considering a change of brake pads or brake shoes, look for its tensioning system. It is a very simple task.

On cable brakes, you just have to tighten the cable, either by means of a screw on the handlebar lever, or by loosening the bolt at the end of the cable to give it more tension.

Picture 101.   Cable crew

Drum brakes are usually tensioned by means of a screw, located close to the drum, called a brake rod.

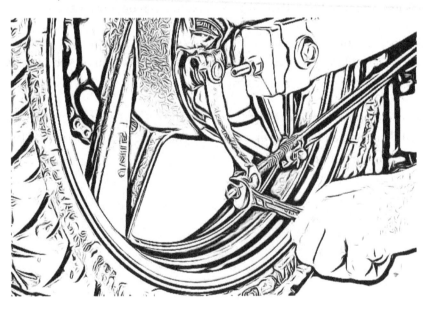

Picture 102.   Drum brake tensioning

Modern hydraulic pumps are equipped with a regulation system, which allows the braking intensity to be adjusted.

Some levers have a numbered wheel that allows more pressure to be applied (more piston travel inside the pump).

Picture 103.   Adjustable brake lever

13 The Electrical System

This is probably the most complicated chapter for me to write.

Electricity is its own specific discipline within mechanics, and there are mechanics and workshops that are dedicated exclusively to electrical issues.

Just as it may seem easy for us to understand how a brake works "because we can see it", we can go our whole lives without understanding how a battery works "because we can't see it with our eyes".

To understand the operation of the electrical components of a motorcycle, some theoretical fundamentals are necessary, which are often not clear even to those who are professionally involved in electricity.

For these reasons, I will try to give this chapter as practical an approach as possible, without getting lost in technicalities or overly theoretical concepts. There will be points where we will err on the side of simplicity, but I would rather do that and get the concept across than lose half of the readers.

We turn on.

13.1 Basic concepts of electricity applied to motorcycles

Direct current or alternating current

I am not going to explain what each current consists of, but it is important to know that the current provided by the **motorcycle battery is direct current**, and the current provided by the alternator (we will see how it works later) is alternating current.

The current that you can find in any socket in your house is always alternating current.

This is because alternating current, unlike direct current, cannot be stored.

All the elements of a motorcycle are designed to operate with direct current, therefore, the electricity produced by the alternator is transformed into direct current by the **rectifier** that all motorcycles have.

Thick or thin cables

This is very simple to understand. The thickness of the cable will always depend on what we find at the end of it.

If it is a light bulb, the wire will be very thin. If it is a starter motor, the wire will be quite thick.

Making a hydraulic simile, for a garden faucet, we need a thin pipe, since it only needs to feed that faucet. If, on the other hand, we look at a ditch in the street, we will see that the pipes are much thicker, since they feed water to many houses.

This is due to resistance. The thinner a cable is, the more resistance it will oppose to the passage of current. If the current to be passed is very little (for example, to power a telltale), the wire can be very thin. If the current is higher (such as to power the starter motor), a thin wire will put up a lot of resistance and heat up, so a thicker wire is necessary.

A cable that is too thin will get hot and may even burn. A thicker cable will only take up more space but will not have any pernicious effect. Never skimp on cable.

Positive pole and negative pole. Ground

We are used to drawing circuits in which a cable leaves the positive pole of the battery, and another cable arrives at the negative pole of the battery. Along the way they feed different elements (light bulbs, engines, etc.).

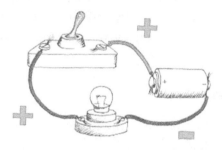

Picture 104.   Traditional circuit

However, we cannot forget that the chassis of a motorcycle is made entirely of metal, and that metals are excellent conductors. For this reason, in motorcycles, one of the two wires is removed from the circuit, and electricity is transmitted through the chassis.

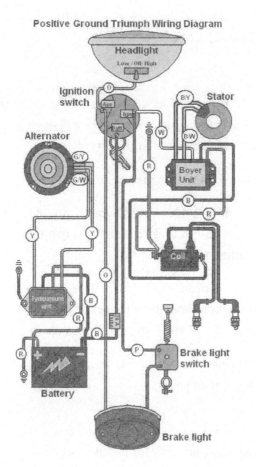

Picture 105.   Wiring diagram of a motorcycle

The chassis of a motorcycle works as a negative pole (almost always, in very few motorcycles it works as a positive pole). This saves half of the cables.

Does this mean that if I touch the chassis, I will get a cramp? Not at all. But if you grab a bare wire coming from the positive pole of the battery and touch the chassis (negative pole), you will be closing the circuit and you will be part of it, so you will get a good shock.

Connecting any element of the motorcycle to the chassis, i.e., attaching it to the negative pole, is called "grounding".

Voltage

Voltage (which is the same as voltage or jump of potential) can be defined as a jump. If the jump is small, we will have a small current. If the jump is large, we will have a large current.

Voltage, as the name implies, is measured in volts.

In our homes we have a 120- or 230-volt jump. It is a relatively large jump that allows us to run a refrigerator, an oven, a washing machine and quite a few other appliances.

On a motorcycle we need much less, some for the turn signals and lights, some for the horn and some more for the starter motor. For this reason, we only need a 12 volt jump.

Older motorcycles needed even less, they didn't even have a starter motor, 6 volts was enough.

Fuses

Electricity is dangerous, not only for people, but also for circuits.

As we have seen before, if we subject a circuit to more current than it is capable of withstanding, it will heat up, even burning.

To avoid this, and to prevent an overvoltage from damaging some other electrical or electronic element (such as the injection control), motorcycles have fuses.

Fuses are nothing more than elements that blow when the current passing through them exceeds the current they are designed for. When they blow, the circuit is cut off, and electricity stops flowing.

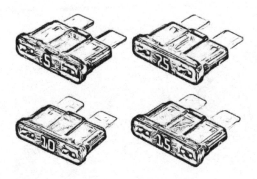

Picture 106.   Fuses of different intensity

When a fuse has blown you have to replace it with a new one (they are cheap, I recommend that you always carry it with you). Before doing so, make sure you have solved the fault that caused the fuse to blow, otherwise it will blow again as soon as you replace it.

13.2 The alternator

With the exception of the battery, the alternator is probably the most important element of a motorcycle's electrical system. It uses the movement of the engine to generate alternating current, which supplies electricity to the motorcycle when it is running.

It is usually housed in a compartment inside the engine, to take advantage of the crankshaft rotation.

In every alternator there is a magnet that rotates to the beat of the engine (called rotor) and a set of coils (coiled copper wires) that surround it, forming a casing around the rotor, called stator. This rotation of a magnet inside a coil generates an alternating current (note to your brother-in-law: this is stated in Faraday's Law).

185

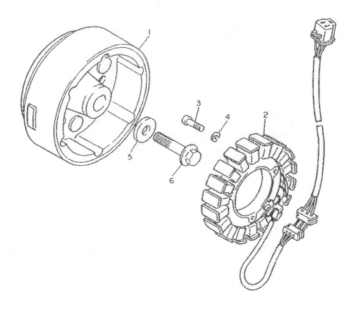

Picture 107.   Alternator

The simplest alternator is the magnetic flywheel, like the one you can see in the picture. It is used in low displacement motorcycles.

In this system, two copper coils are usually installed. One for ignition and one for lighting.

The coils are static, but the flywheel rotates with the crankshaft. Two magnets are housed in the flywheel (rotor), so their rotation causes the direction of the magnetic field on the coils to change. This is what generates the alternating current necessary for all the electrical elements of the motorcycle and to charge the battery.

13.3 The regulator or rectifier

We have already produced electricity in the alternator.

However, we have two drawbacks:

1) It is alternate; therefore, we cannot store it.
2) Its tension depends on the crankshaft speed.

For this reason, it is necessary to insert an element called a rectifier (also known as a diode plate).

The rectifier transforms the alternating current into direct current, valid for charging the battery.

This solves the first drawback.

In order to achieve a stable voltage that does not depend on the speed of engine rotation, regulators are installed.

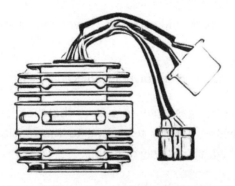

Picture 108.   Regulator/rectifier

13.4 The battery

As we have seen, the alternator generates current as the crankshaft rotates. However, what happens when the bike is at a standstill?

At that moment we could not use any electrical element, not even start the motorcycle if it has a starter motor.

That is what the battery is for.

The battery is charged by the current generated by the alternator, which must pass through the rectifier and the regulator before reaching the battery.

The energy capacity that a battery can accumulate is measured in Ampere-hours (A-h).

If your battery has 30 A-h it means it can provide a current of 30 amps in one hour, or 10 amps in 3 hours.

The battery is made up of metal plates (they used to be made of lead but are gradually being replaced by nickel and cadmium plates). They also contain a liquid called electrolyte (sulfuric acid and distilled water).

This liquid is highly toxic and corrosive, so you must handle it with great care.

In modern batteries this electrolyte is replaced by a gel.

In order to allow the gases generated by the chemical reactions that take place inside the battery to escape to the outside, batteries are usually equipped with a spillway or drain.

By the way, the vast majority of today's motorcycle batteries are 12V.

13.5 The ignition system

The ignition system is the system that generates the spark needed at the spark plug to get everything going.

The source of electricity to produce the spark is clear: the alternator and the battery.

We lack a system that makes the spark appear just at the precise moment when the piston is at its highest point (TDC) and the intake and exhaust valves are closed. This is done by the ignition.

> *Actually, the spark must occur a little before TDC, in what we know as ignition advance, but let's leave it that way so as not to overcomplicate the explanation.*

This is achieved by means of platinum or electronic ignition.

Contact point

This is a system used on older motorcycles, clearly in danger of extinction.

The system is based on the existence of two contacts which join and separate as the crankshaft turns.

When the TDC is reached, the contacts separate, causing the current generated to be diverted to the spark plug, producing the spark.

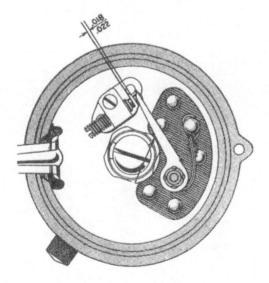

Picture 109.   Contact point open 0.022 inch

I try to assimilate everything related to electricity to hydraulics, which is much more intuitive for me.

Imagine a hose to which we have made a small hole, so small that while the faucet is open, the water comes out of the mouth of the hose without us noticing any leakage.

The "easy" path for the water is to exit through the mouth of the hose (with the sinkers closed (i.e., glued) the current passes through them as this is its "easiest" path).

If we cover the mouth of the hose without closing the faucet, the water will look for a way, even if it is more difficult. At that moment the water will come out through the small hole (with the contacts open, the current has no choice but to look for another way, which is none other than the wire that ends in the spark plug, producing the spark).

This occurs at each revolution of the engine, always at the same moment, producing the explosion of the mixture in the cylinder.

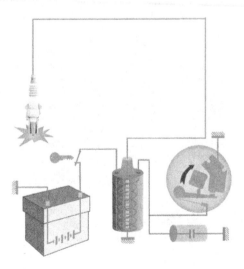

Picture 110.   Open contact point: spark is produced

Contact point is a system in disuse because they wear out and it is necessary to adjust the gap between them from time to time.

The spark plug needs a very high voltage to produce the spark (more than 10,000 V). This is achieved by inserting a new coil that raises the voltage and lowers the current. It is called high coil.

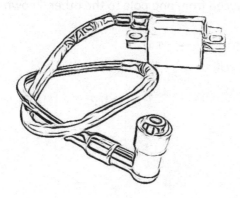

Picture 111.   High coil with spark plug pipe

Electronic ignition

Nowadays you do not have to be an experienced mechanic to get the spark plug on your motorcycle to jump at the right time.

Fortunately, there is also no maintenance required to ensure that the ignition is tight.

Since the invention of electronic ignition, the signal for the spark to jump at the spark plug at the exact moment is sent by transmitters or control units, which are precisely configured at the factory.

This is what we know as CDI (Capacitor Discharge Induction) systems.

The basis of the CDI is the induction of current by a capacitor.

13.6 The spark plug

The spark plug is the element in charge of generating the spark that causes the explosion of the air-gasoline mixture.

The spark is produced when a potential difference is generated between the ends of two electrodes (one is inside the spark plug and the other at the end that is introduced into the engine). At that moment a "jump" of electrons is produced from one pole to the other, known as electric arc.

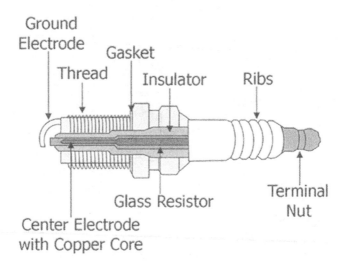

Picture 112.   Parts of a spark plug

The spark plug is supplied with current through a wire attached to a terminal commonly called a "pipe".

In its highest part there is a threaded terminal (the screw cap must be removed to connect the pipe). Behind this terminal there is a white porcelain area, which acts as an electrical insulator.

In the lower part of the spark plug there is an area that is screwed into the cylinder head to ensure sealing.

The part inside the cylinder head contains the two electrodes, the center electrode and the ground electrode. The spark is produced between them.

A voltage of more than 10,000 V is produced in the spark plug, so be careful when testing it if you don't want to get a good shock.

✗ Fitting a spark plug

Removing and inserting a spark plug is a very common operation to do on your motorcycle.

The color of the spark plug is a great indicator of the health of your engine, but to check it, you must first remove the spark plug.

To do so, use a specific spark plug wrench like the one in the picture.

Picture 113.   Spark plug wrench

Spark plug identification

Each bike has its own spark plug. You can find differences in all this:

- 🔧 **Thread**: the most common diameters are 14 and 10 mm, however, there are also 8, 12 and 18 mm threads.
- 🔧 **The neck**: there are short neck (12.7 mm) and long neck (19 mm) spark plugs. This is the length of the part that is inserted

into the cylinder head. If you overdo it, the spark plug can hit the piston, causing serious damage.

- 🏍 **Temperature**: cold spark plugs evacuate heat quickly and are recommended for engines with high compression. Hot spark plugs are recommended for engines with lower performance, as they ensure that the entire mixture is burned by maintaining a higher temperature.

Unfortunately, each brand uses its own nomenclature, so it is impossible to know all the data of a spark plug without having the brand guide at hand.

Picture 114.   NGK spark plug

For example, in the picture we have an NGK 7162DR8EA spark plug.

- 🏍 D: indicates the diameter of the thread. 12 mm.
- 🏍 A: it is a resistance spark plug.
- 🏍 8: is the thermal rating. The higher the number, the colder the spark plug. Very intuitive...
- 🏍 E: neck length. This is a 19 mm spark plug.
- 🏍 A: indicates the type of seat. Flat in this case.

If we look for the equivalent spark plug in Bosh, we find the XR4CC. As you can see, the code looks like an egg to a chestnut.

Picture 115.   Bosh spark plug

- 🏍 The X indicates the dimensions. In this case a 12mm diameter thread and 1.5mm thread pitch.
- 🏍 The R indicates an antiparasitic resistance.
- 🏍 The 4 indicates the thermal degree but be careful! At Bosch, the lower the number, the colder the spark plug.
- 🏍 The first C indicates that the length of the neck is 19 mm.
- 🏍 The second C tells us that the electrodes are copper.

As you can see, it is not worth learning the codes until the manufacturers agree.

What does the color of a spark plug indicate?

Fever in humans is a symptom that something is wrong. As soon as we notice that our temperature rises, we run to the doctor or pharmacy to remedy something that affects us.

With our motorcycles the same thing happens, the spark plug is not usually the problem, however, it is usually a great indicator of the health of our engine. That is why it is important to learn how to read the color of a motorcycle spark plug.

Grayish white or light brown

If the base of the insulator (the white part) has a dirty white, yellowish or light brown color, the spark plug is functioning properly.

This is the color that a motorcycle spark plug should have.

The engine is correctly calibrated, as well as the carburetion, and the spark plug heat rating is ideal.

It is also normal for the external electrode to have a whitish color.

Spark plug covered with dry black soot

Color: it is a common coloration when you are restoring an old motorcycle. The spark plug appears totally black, with a powdery residue, which disappears when wiped with a cloth.

Problem: we will have problems starting the bike when cold, which will fail at slow speed or idle. False explosions.

Causes:

- 🏍 Mixture too rich in gasoline.
- 🏍 The ignition timing may be retarded (the spark is produced when the piston is already down).
- 🏍 The thermal rating of the spark plug is too cold.
- 🏍 The air filter is dirty.
- 🏍 The ignition voltage is not correct.
- 🏍 The choke is not well regulated.
- 🏍 The engine has been running at low rpm for a long time.

<u>Wet gasoline spark plug</u>

Color: the spark plug is impregnated with gasoline.

Problem: the bike does not start well and, when it does, it does not run well at idle speed.

Causes:

- 🏍 The engine is choked.
- 🏍 Spark plug electrodes are too far apart or too close together. Spark does not jump.

Spark plug with white, yellowish or reddish deposits

Color: the spark plug appears to be oxidized or with colored residues (white, yellow, red, brown) covering it. They disappear when wiped with a cloth.

Problem: Engine misfires at high rpm, loses power. The combustion of these particles can cause engine damage.

Causes:

- 🏍 Check the quality of the gasoline, it may contain additives that are depositing on the spark plug.
- 🏍 Check the fuel filter to ensure that no residue enters the carburetor.
- 🏍 The oil may have impurities that do not burn.

<u>Black spark plug with wet appearance</u>

Color: unlike soot, it is a shiny, wet black, which covers the electrodes.

Problem: we will have problems starting the motorcycle, which will fail at slow speed or idle.

Causes: oil in the combustion chamber.

- 🏍 The piston rings are not in good condition and the lubrication oil rises into the combustion chamber.
- 🏍 Valve seals in bad condition.
- 🏍 Cylinder in bad condition. It may be necessary to rectify it.
- 🏍 If the engine is a two-stroke engine, excess oil in the mixture.

<u>Spark plug with bright insulator with granules</u>

Color: the tip of the insulator is too bright, yellowish or light brown, with dark granules.

Problem: the engine fails when it is heavily stressed, when accelerating or going uphill.

Causes: overheated spark plug.

- 🏍 Advanced ignition: the spark jumps before the piston is fully raised.
- 🏍 Poor mixture, with excess air vs. gasoline.
- 🏍 Overheated engine, which does not cool well.
- 🏍 Low octane fuel.
- 🏍 Excessive heat rating spark plug.

Yellow spark plug

Color: the insulator tip is covered by a yellowish, brownish or even greenish layer. This is a lead film, which does not disappear when wiped with a cloth.

Problem: the engine misfires when heavily stressed, when accelerating or climbing. The spark plug was replaced 1,500 mi ago (2.000 km).

Causes:

- 🏍 Lead additives in the fuel. They have not been consumed as the spark plug has been operated at partial speed. The spark plug must be replaced.

Spark plug with ash

Color: it is not only black soot, but a thick layer of whitish or grayish ash.

Problem: false explosions and loss of power.

Causes:

- 🏍 Oil components or additives generate ash that accumulates in the combustion chamber.

Fused center electrode

Appearance: the central electrode appears melted or semi-melted, with the insulator surrounding it softened or in poor condition.

Problem: misfiring and loss of power.

The spark plugs must be replaced.

Causes:

- 🏍 Incorrectly adjusted ignition (normally advanced).
- 🏍 Combustion residues in the chamber.
- 🏍 Valves in bad condition.
- 🏍 Spark plug heat rating too high. Spark plug too hot.
- 🏍 Fuel in poor condition or very poor mixture.
- 🏍 Poorly tightened spark plug.

Molten electrodes

Appearance: electrodes appear melted or badly worn.

Problems: difficulty or impossibility to start and failure to accelerate.

Causes:

- 🏍 Very aggressive additives in the fuel or oil.
- 🏍 Engine pitting.
- 🏍 Deposits in the combustion chamber.
- 🏍 Spark plug too hot.

13.7 Lighting and signage

Lights are useful to see at night, but above all to be seen.

The lights of a motorcycle are one of the elements that must have its own homologation code to be obtained by the manufacturer. This should give us an idea of their importance. We cannot change them for ones without a homologation code.

Bulb types

Motorcycles can be fitted with incandescent or LED bulbs. By the way, it is correct to call them lamps, not bulbs.

The basis of the former is to pass an electric current (direct or alternating, it doesn't matter) through a tungsten filament (also called tungsten). When it becomes incandescent (red hot), it generates a beam of light.

Nowadays most incandescent lamps are halogen. This means that a halogen gas is introduced into the glass bulb. These lamps last longer than conventional lamps, but also consume more energy.

By the way, you should not touch the bulb of a halogen lamp. The quartz glass can be damaged by sweat, grease or dirt on your hand. This does not happen with conventional lamps or LEDs.

LED lamps achieve the same luminous intensity with a much lower power consumption.

It is important to note that you cannot change a halogen lamp to LED. It is forbidden. This is because the headlamp is designed for a specific type of lamp. It would be necessary to change the complete optics, and this requires a homologation procedure.

Yes, you can change a complete headlight, or whole turn signals. Of course, you will have to homologate them if you want to pass the ITV.

There are many types of lamps that are identified by a sequence of numbers and letters. Each motorcycle can be fitted with a different lamp.

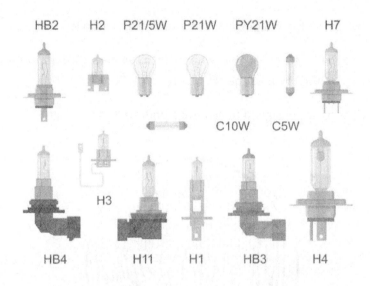

Picture 116.   Types of lamps on a motorcycle

Headlight

It is the main lighting element of a motorcycle. Normally there is only one headlight on the motorcycle, however, there are motorcycles that mount several headlights.

The headlight includes 3 lights as mandatory:

- 🏍 **Position light**: it is used to be seen. It must be turned on when the motorcycle is started.
- 🏍 **Low beam**: these are known as dipped headlights. They are currently mandatory for driving even during the day. Unlike the

rest, they are not symmetrical with respect to the longitudinal plane of the motorcycle to avoid glare. In countries where you drive on the right, the beam of light shines to the right and vice versa.

🛵 **High beam**: the main beam. For use at night when there is no danger of dazzling other drivers.

If you notice, all the headlights have a curved and grooved surface.

The curvature is to avoid that when light rays pass through the glass, they are directed towards the sky due to refraction.

The striations are designed to achieve a uniform beam of light.

Picture 117.   Striations on a headlight

Tail light

This element also has two lights: position light and brake light. Sometimes it also serves as a license plate light.

In this case, the pilot usually has a single bulb with two filaments. One of higher power (usually 21w) to warn that we are braking, and another of lower power (usually 5w) for the position and license plate light.

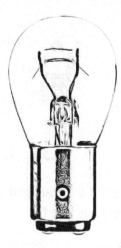

Picture 118.   Double filament lamp

Although it can be independent, the mandatory retro-reflector is also usually located on the tail lamp. This is a red element that reflects the light of other vehicles approaching from behind.

Turn signals

In the past they were not mandatory, in fact, it is common to find classic motorcycles that do not have them, however, nowadays all motorcycles must have 4 turn signals.

I imagine you know this, but to signal which way the motorcycle was going to turn, there was a system of arm signs that must have been curious to see.

Picture 119.   Motorcycle sign language

Unlike other lights, turn signals are equipped with a device that makes them turn on and off continuously: the flasher relay.

It is a plastic canister with 3 legs:

- 🏍 One is connected to the power supply (B)
- 🏍 Another with the flasher knob or switch (L)
- 🏍 Another one goes to mass (E)

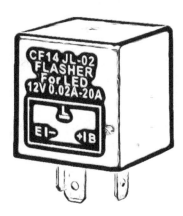

Picture 120.   Flasher relay

A word of advice: if a relay starts to fail, buy a new one. They are very cheap and, although you can check if they work with a multimeter, these checks can give false results and are not worth the savings.

If you've ever wondered, the blinking frequency is regulated by regulation, and must be **between 60 and 120 times per minute.**

The maximum power of a flasher is usually 21w.

Other lights

On a motorcycle we can find other lights, some of them mandatory and others optional:

- 🏍 **Catadioptric**: these are those red elements that reflect the light of other vehicles. They are passive safety elements; they are used to be seen. At least one rear one is mandatory. They are usually located under the license plate or integrated in the rear light.
- 🏍 **License plate light**: it is used to illuminate the license plate when the motorcycle lights are on. It is mandatory and can be independent or integrated in the tail light.
- 🏍 **Fog lights**: these are optional and are installed to provide better illumination in foggy conditions.
- 🏍 **Witnesses**: small colored lamps that are usually installed inside the speedometer itself or on the dashboard. They give an indication of the oil temperature, which lights are on or if the motorcycle is in neutral.

13.8 The starter motor

When we talked about starting the bike, I told you that there are 3 ways to do it: kick start, push start and engine starter.

Obviously the cleanest and most convenient way is to press the button that activates the starter motor.

Its operation is very simple. It is an electric engine that rotates the crankshaft, making the pistons start to move up and down until a spark makes the whole system start up.

To work, it needs to be connected to a fully charged battery. As the most consuming electrical element on a motorcycle, it will be the first to be affected if the battery starts to fail or becomes slightly discharged.

Picture 121.   Section of a starter motor

The starter motor only works when we press the button that activates it.

Once we release the button, even if the bike has started, it stops driving the gear that ultimately moves the piston. This disconnection of the starter motor is handled by the Bendix.

13.9 The switchboard

The control unit is the computer that controls the electrical and electronic system of our motorcycles.

It is a set of chips and integrated circuits enclosed in a plastic box, usually black in color.

Before the advent of ECUs, motorcycles began to be fitted with a device called ECU (Engine Control Unit). Its purpose was to comply with increasingly restrictive exhaust emission regulations.

The most important element inside the control unit is the CDI (Capacitor Discharge Ignition), which is responsible for producing the spark plug spark at the right time.

In today's motorcycles, the control unit not only controls the ignition, but also conditions a series of electrical characteristics of the motorcycle, ranging from engine power, consumption, the cooling system, temperature and battery charge.

13.10 Common electrical system malfunctions

1) Blown fuses

In the event of any electrical malfunction of our motorcycle, we must first go to the fuse box (or to the fuse, if the motorcycle has only one).

It is usually under the seat, but every bike is different, so I recommend you check the manual.

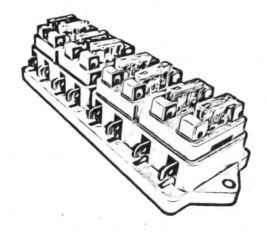

Picture 122.　　Fuse box

Checking if a fuse is blown is very simple, just remove it from its box and see if the central wire is continuous or broken.

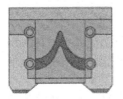 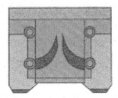

Picture 123.　　Fuse in good condition and blown fuse

Each fuse has a number, which marks the intensity in amperes that can pass through the circuit it protects.

You should not replace a fuse with a higher amperage fuse to stop it from blowing, because you will cause the circuit to blow before the fuse that protects it.

Before replacing a fuse, make sure that the fault that caused the fuse to blow is resolved. Otherwise, it will blow again immediately.

Fuses are cheap, I recommend that you always carry a good collection on your motorcycle.

2) Power supply problem

When a particular electrical element of your motorcycle stops working overnight (for example, the horn), the first thing to check is the continuity of the circuit that supplies it.

That is to say, it receives current.

To do this, the easiest way is to get another battery (or the same battery from your bike if you don't have another one at hand) and power the element directly with two cables.

If the horn sounds, the bulb lights up or the starter motor starts, you will know immediately that you have a continuity problem in the circuit.

Then perform the following checks:

a. Check that you do not have a blown fuse.
b. Check that cable and element connections are tight and clean.
c. Check the continuity of the chassis. To do this, power the element with a positive pole and connect the negative to the chassis. If it does not work, there is no power to that part of the chassis.
d. Finally, check the wiring with a multimeter.

3) Melted light ✖

It is the most common breakdown in any vehicle, with the exception of punctures.

You have no choice but to replace the lamp that has blown (its filament has broken) with another of the same characteristics.

Each bike has a different way to disassemble the headlight or pilot, sometimes you will have to remove a fairing, but it is always easier than it seems.

If leaving the bulb in plain sight becomes a very complex task, there's probably some trick you've overlooked. It should be in the instruction manual.

4) Veiled or opaque glass of a lighthouse

The prolonged action of the sun on the headlamps causes them to lose their transparency, becoming whitish and translucent crystals.

In addition to losing lighting efficiency, it is a fault that can cause your motorcycle to fail the MOT.

You can remedy this with very fine water sandpaper and polish.

Here are the steps to polish the headlight of your motorcycle:

1. Start by masking off the parts you don't want to polish, such as the bezel of your headlight. Do this with masking tape.
2. Apply 800 grit sandpaper (wet in water) to the headlight.
3. Do the same next with a 1200 grit.
4. Finish with a 2000 grain.
5. Apply polish with a chamois and rub in circles with force.
6. Clean with a cloth and water.

Your headlight will be as good as new.

5) Starter motor does nothing

Few things can spoil your day as much as getting to your bike, pressing the starter button and not hearing a single click.

In such cases, you must perform all of these checks:

1. The kickstand is securely retracted.
2. The power cut-off button is not pressed.
3. There is no gear engaged and you are not depressing the clutch (some motorcycles do not allow starting if they are not in neutral).

After ruling out all "silly" faults we must check if the bike has a battery. A simple activation of the horn or lights should suffice.

After this we will check if there is power to the starter motor. Locate the wires that feed the starter motor and, using a multimeter, place one terminal in the positive pole and another one in any point of the chassis. Press the starter button and check for current.

Locate the fuse box and check that the fuse protecting the starter motor is not blown.

Another way to rule out an internal starter failure is to power the starter directly from the battery, i.e., pull two wires directly from the battery and connect them to the starter terminals. The negative pole can be the starter body itself.

Finally, another element that often causes electrical faults in the starter motor is its relay. Test it and check if the engine responds in this way.

If we rule out power failure, which is the most common fault, we will have no choice but to disassemble the starter motor and take it to be repaired or replaced, as it is a serious fault.

6) Battery does not charge

One of the most common failures of the electrical system is running out of battery.

Batteries have a useful life of about 2-3 years, so after that time we will have no choice but to buy a new battery.

However, sometimes it can happen that our motorcycle does not charge the battery, constantly running out of power and having to resort to a battery charger.

As we have seen, the battery is charged with the current generated by the alternator, which must pass through the rectifier (to switch from AC to DC) and the regulator (to avoid current peaks) before reaching the battery.

To check if this system is charging the battery of our motorcycle, we will make the following checks:

a) Observe if the generator light turns off when the engine revs up.

Some motorcycles have a telltale that measures the health of the charging system. It is usually a small battery or the letters GEN (for generator). This light should turn off when we reach certain revolutions, synonymous that the battery is charging.

On the move it may turn on if the battery is depleted or if there is a problem with the charging system.

b) Measure if the battery voltage rises when we increase revolutions.

For this we will need a voltmeter. Place one terminal on each pole of the battery, without disconnecting them from the motorcycle.

Accelerate hard. If the voltage rises as you accelerate, you know that power is flowing into the battery.

Picture 124.   Load check on Azahara, my BMW R45

c) Check the operation of the load indication system. To do this, check the alternator continuity by placing the multimeter terminals of the first brush to ground.
d) Confirm rotor continuity.
e) Check the brushes for wear.
f) Check if the regulator works. To do this, bypass it and check if the voltage rises when accelerating.

7) No spark at spark plug

When a motorcycle does not start, one of the first things to check is to remove the spark plug, place it on a metal surface (usually on the cylinder head) and, without removing it from its pipe, press the starter button or press the pedal.

If a bright spark does not appear we have a problem.

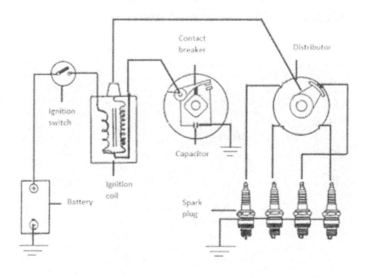

Picture 125.   Electrical diagram of a spark plug

The sequence of checks is as follows:

a. Check that the ignition is turned on and the starter lock is not pressed.

b. If the bike has more than one cylinder: is there spark on other spark plugs? If there is no spark on any spark plug, your problem will be "upstream" of the coils. If all the spark plugs have spark except one, the problem is in the distributor, the coil, the pipe or the spark plug itself.

c. Try another spark plug that you know gives spark. Spark plugs are cheap, don't waste time checking the whole circuit if you have doubts that the problem is in the spark plug itself.

d. Check the condition of the pipe. It is common for the connection to loosen. This connection can be threaded, or press fit.

Picture 126.   Spark plug pipe

e. Measure the continuity in the wire connecting the pipe and the coil.
f. Check the high voltage coil. To do this, with a multimeter, first measure the continuity:

    a. On the primary coil (place the multimeter terminals on the two input legs of the coil). There should be continuity.

    b. There must be no continuity between the ground input and the output to the pipe.

g. Check the resistance of the coil. To do this, place the multimeter in the resistance (Ω) position:
   a. Primary winding: 200 ohms scale. The primary coil has to be in a range between 0.2 and 3 ohms.
   b. Secondary winding. Scale 20,000 ohms. The secondary coil needs to be in the 5k to 20k ohms range, although this may vary depending on your bike.

h. If everything checked is correct, the next step is the ignition, which can vary greatly depending on your bike and is far from a basic mechanics book.

8) Turn signals do not blink

A very common electrical malfunction is for the turn signals to remain fixed, or to flash at the wrong rate.

In that case, after checking that none of the flasher lights are fused, we will have to check the flasher relay.

When a relay starts to fail, I always recommend replacing it, they are inexpensive and not worth repairing.

9) Battery replacement 🔧

A conventional motorcycle battery lasts approximately 2-3 years.

From then on, one day, when you go to start the bike, you may be unpleasantly surprised to find that it won't start. It does nothing.

Although you can charge it with an external charger, if there are no other faults on your motorcycle, it is normal that the battery has reached the end of its useful life and it is time to replace it.

Changing a battery is a very simple task:

1) Locate it: if you have never changed the battery of your motorcycle, this may be the most complicated task. On road motorcycles it is located in the central part of the motorcycle, approximately under the seat, housed in the central part of the chassis. On a scooter it is usually found under one of the supports where you place your feet.
2) Open its compartment.
3) Disconnect the negative pole terminal: this is very important, otherwise you will get a good shock.
4) Disconnect the positive pole terminal: always after disconnecting the negative pole.
5) Remove the battery and purchase it, otherwise it will probably not fit in the compartment.

To mount it the order is the opposite, i.e., first tighten the positive pole and then the negative. This way there is no risk of cramps.

In the past, the life of a battery could be extended by replacing distilled water. Nowadays batteries are usually gel or maintenance-free, so it is necessary to buy a new one.

14 Suspension

Riding a motorcycle without suspension would become an ordeal. Although the roads are getting better and better, having a system to mitigate road irregularities is a must.

This has not always been the case, since the first motorcycles did not have shock absorbers, although they were soon installed, even if only under the seat.

A motorcycle always has two suspensions, front and rear, and we will study them separately, as they have very different characteristics.

The basis of any suspension system is the spring, a well-known helical element that tends to recover its initial length when the force applied to it ceases.

14.1 Front suspension

The front shock absorber system par excellence is the telescopic fork.

This system, present on all motorcycles, consists of two independent arms, joined at the top by the seat posts and at the bottom by the front wheel axle.

Inside each of the arms there are two bars, one of which is thinner, allowing one to be inserted inside the other. Damping is provided by a long spring inside.

If the damping were limited to a single spring, every time we braked or cleared an obstacle, the bike would pitch and roll until the spring stabilized. It would be quite a comical situation to watch from the outside, but insufferable for the rider.

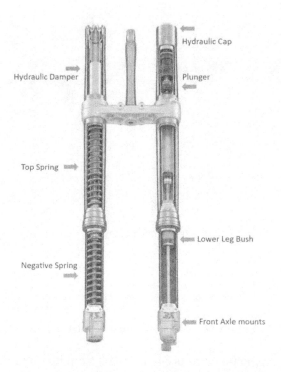

Hydraulic Cap

Hydraulic Damper

Plunger

Top Spring

Negative Spring

Lower Leg Bush

Front Axle mounts

Picture 127.　　　Fork parts (inverted)

To avoid this infinite oscillation of the spring, the so-called hydraulic brake is introduced. This system is nothing more than a perforated disc that must move through an oily medium. In order for the disc to move, the oil must pass through its holes, which causes a much more gradual movement.

To understand it well, we can imagine jumping into a pool with or without water. In both cases we can reach the bottom, but it is clear that the result will not be the same. The oil in the suspension bottle acts as the water in the pool, cushioning the movement of the spring.

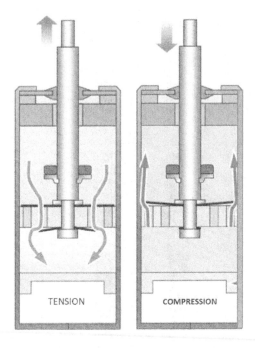

Picture 128.   Hydraulic suspension operation

Rubber seals are installed to prevent the oil from leaking out of the fork bottle and must be changed periodically.

In the usual telescopic fork system, the bottle is located at the bottom, and the suspension rods are attached to the upper stem, however, it is increasingly common to find inverted forks, in which the system is arranged the other way around. This results in stiffer systems, much appreciated in sporty riding.

If you struggle to differentiate between them, think that in a conventional fork the seals face upwards, in an inverted fork they will face the ground.

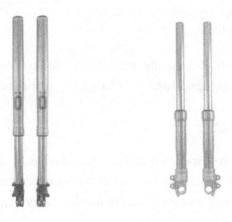

Picture 129.   Inverted fork vs. normal fork

🛠 Change of suspension seals

The retainer is a cylindrical piece of plastic material that seals the fork bottle, preventing suspension fluid from escaping.

Picture 130.   Fork seal

It is an element subjected to continuous friction, so it is common that over time it ends up allowing a small amount of oil to leak out, very easily detectable in the chrome-plated suspension rods.

When this occurs, it is advisable to change the oil seals.

When the leakage is abundant, it can even stain the brake pads, severely affecting braking.

To change the seals, it is usually necessary to disassemble the fork rods, so we must take the opportunity to change the suspension oil.

✖ Fork oil change

The most common suspension maintenance task is to change the oil in the telescopic fork. This is an oil that degrades over time and should be replaced after about 2 years of heavy use (or every 15,000 mi / 25.000 km).

For this purpose, the fork bottles have a bleeder at the bottom, through which you can drain the old liquid. Modern bottles do not usually have this bleeder, which makes the process more complicated (you have to disassemble the bars).

Personally, it is not something I like to do myself. It requires a lot of time and patience and is not too expensive in a workshop (about 150 €). However, I will tell you the steps to follow:

1) Make sure that the bike has a good support. When removing the fork, the bike will inevitably pitch over the triple clamp.
2) You must disassemble the fork rods. To do this, first remove the wheel, front fender, brake calipers and speedometer cable. Some motorcycles allow you to do the process without disassembling the bar completely, but here I am going to tell you the general procedure.
3) Remove the suspension rod cap. Do this before releasing the bar from the triple clamp. This way the triple clamp itself will act as a bar clamp. Be careful because the plug may come out under pressure.
4) Loosen the bolts on the seat posts that hold the bars together.
5) Dismount the bar from the motorcycle.

6) Pour the used oil into a container, without removing the spring from the cartridge. Pull the spring or rod in and out of the bottle to expel all the oil.

7) Carefully remove the dust covers and the circlip retainers. Do this with a flat-blade screwdriver with a low cutting edge. It is essential that you do not scratch the fork leg. Write down or take pictures of the order of the parts. The usual order will be:
    a. Overalls.
    b. Clip or circlip.
    c. Retainer (this will be removed in the next point).
    d. Bushing.

8) Pull the cartridge rod out of the fork by pulling it forcefully outward. This will also remove the retainer. Make sure you have loosened the bolt at the base of the fork beforehand.

9) It is essential to replace oil seals and dust covers with new ones. Reassemble them in the same order.

10) Fill with new fluid, following the manufacturer's measurements.

11) Compress the fork until the oil completely fills the hydraulics. Leave the fork fully compressed.

12) Close the plugs again and ride the motorcycle.

14.2 Rear suspension

If in the front damping we had the problem of sharing the need to dampen with the need to turn (a system that did not influence the steering while damping was required), in the rear axle suspension and secondary transmission have to coexist.

Any movement of the wheel will inevitably generate a movement on the transmission (chain, belt or cardan), causing stresses in the system.

This is solved with the incorporation of the swingarm, a system that ensures that the distance between the rear wheel axle and the attack pinion (gear that transmits the movement to the chain or belt), or cardan anchor is invariable.

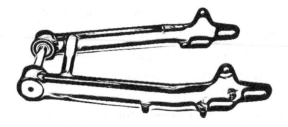

Picture 131.   Swingarm

The swingarm is nothing more than a rigid structure attached to the chassis by an axle, which allows free movement around that axis, which coincides (or almost coincides) with the axis of the attack pinion. The rear wheel is anchored to this structure.

To achieve rear damping, one or two robust springs are inserted between the chassis and the swingarm, thus damping any movement of the swingarm, and therefore of the rear wheel.

As in the front suspension, the springs can be accompanied by a hydraulic retention system. Rear shock absorbers, in addition to oil, may be retained by pressurized gas, usually nitrogen.

The gas increases its volume when heated, which is why this type of system usually has reservoirs external to the damper, on the one hand, to allow the gas to expand and, on the other hand, to cool it.

Rear shock absorbers are usually adjustable, usually by means of springs that pre-compress the spring, making the system more rigid.

Picture 132.   Nitrogen shock absorber

On older motorcycles, it was very common to find single-seater seats with large springs underneath.

This was because motorcycles normally did not have rear suspension, so all the damping was on the seat.

Even the seat was spring formed.

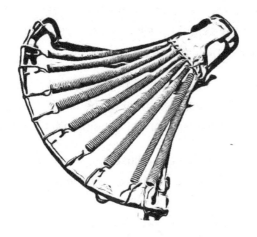

Picture 133.   Spring seat

15 The Horn

It may seem like a minor component, but the horn of a motorcycle can get us out of more than one trouble (besides alerting our girlfriend or boyfriend to get out of the house).

The truth is that it is a component that, when it breaks down, is usually replaced, since they are not expensive. It must also be said that it is not a component that usually breaks down. They are extremely watertight, and their operation is very simple, so they do not usually cause problems.

Its operation is based on a thin metallic membrane that vibrates, producing a sound. When receiving electric current (when we press the horn button), the coil or winding inside the horn generates an electromagnetic field that separates a metal disc (diffuser disc) from the membrane that produces the sound.

When it is free, it can vibrate, and that is when the sound is produced. When we stop pressing the button, the current disappears, and the metal disc stops the vibration of the membrane.

As mentioned above, a horn requires very little maintenance or repair. In case it does not emit any sound, check that it receives current when pressing the button, in the vast majority of the occasions, the cause of the failure will be due to a lack of electrical current. In the rest of the cases, the entry of water into the compartment that houses all the machinery will have oxidized some element.

If you want to check that your horn works, you just have to feed it with two cables directly from the battery, one from the positive pole, and one from the negative pole (or directly with a cable to the chassis).

Another maintenance task of the horn is its **tuning**. If you detect that the sound it emits is not adequate, just tighten or loosen the nut on the back of the horn.

16 Chassis

The chassis is the support of the motorcycle, its structure, the canvas on which the rest of the components are placed.

It consists of a set of steel tubes or bars (although they can also be made of aluminum) with supports for the most important elements of the motorcycle, which are anchored to the chassis:

- Engine
- Front fork
- Swingarm
- Rear shock absorbers
- Seat

The swingarm is the part that supports the rear axle with the rear wheel and owes its name to the fact that it "tilts" over the chassis, allowing the suspension of the rear wheel.

The subframe is the part attached to the chassis by bolts or welding that holds the seat, and therefore the rider.

The chassis is not an element that requires any mechanical knowledge (beyond that of course for those who design the bike) or any particular maintenance, apart from keeping it clean and painted to avoid corrosion.

As a curiosity, in 1967 Ossa presented its sadly famous Ossa 250 Monocoque, the bike on which the famous rider Santiago Herrero lost his life in the Isle of Man Tourist Trophy.

It was a motorcycle with a chassis made of magnesium sheet metal, which integrated the tank inside the chassis itself. It weighed 20 kg less than the rest of its competitors, which gave it a huge advantage.

17 Maintenance of Your Motorcycle

I wanted to leave for the end (so that you always have it at hand) the maintenance tasks that you should perform to keep your bike always in perfect condition.

As with everything described in this book, there will be some that you can do yourself, and others that you will have to do in a workshop. If you are reading this book, I am sure you will try to carry out almost all of them yourself.

In the table you will be able to check the maintenance tasks that you should do to your motorcycle, as you go riding miles.

These are indicative periods, which may vary with your motorcycle model. Ideally, always consult the manual for your specific motorcycle.

They can also vary depending on the type of riding or the environment in which you use the motorcycle (dusty roads, very hot areas, only in the city, etc.).

I have included the page of the book where you can find how to do the specific maintenance of that element.

Frequency	Maintenance task	Page
Every 300 mi / 500 km	Tire check	153
	Lubrication and chain tensioning	117
	Oil and brake fluid levels	67/174
	Spoke tension	
	General cleaning of the motorcycle	
Every 3,000 mi 5.000 km	Oil and filter change	67
	Check spark plugs	195
	Check air filter	132
	Carburetor synchronization	127
	Clutch cable overhaul	119
	Overhaul of wheel bearings	
	Coolant check	79
	Screw adjustment	
	Stand overhaul	
	Battery charge check	217
	Tightening of the steering	
	Overhaul of steering bearings	
Every 6,000 mi 10.000 km	Gasoline filter change	
	Overhaul of swingarm bearings	
	Changing the air filter	132
Every 9,000 mi 15.000 km	Brake pad replacement	169
Every 15,000 mi 25.000 km	Brake fluid change	174
	Coolant change	
	Fork oil change	228
	Valve adjustment	93
	Change of the sprocket kit	118
Every 18,000 mi 30.000 km	Spark plug replacement	195
Every 35,000 mi 60.000 km	Brake disc replacement	173
Every 125,000 mi 200.000 km	Replacement of the distribution kit	

18 Farewell

I loved writing this book.

I have learned a lot of things that I did not know, it has helped me to consolidate my knowledge and I have corrected old vices that I had acquired by doing things without knowing the theory.

I have enjoyed imagining each task from home, waiting for the weekend to arrive so I could put it into practice.

I hope it has helped you and that it has awakened your interest for mechanics.

I hope this book ends up full of grease, with a torn page stored under the seat of a motorcycle or punctured in the cork of the garage.

It will have been worth it.

Thank you very much for having made it this far.

A big hug,

Rafa Moreno.

19 Index of Images

20 Mechanical Notes